Fortress • 18

Norman Stone Castles (2)

Europe 950–1204

Christopher Gravett • Illustrated by Adam Hook

Series editors Marcus Cowper and Nikolai Bogdanovic

First published in Great Britain in 2004 by Osprey Publishing,
Midland House, West Way, Botley, Oxford OX2 0PH, United Kingdom.
443 Park Avenue South, New York, NY 10016, USA
Email: info@ospreypublishing.com
© 2004 Osprey Publishing Ltd.

ISBN 1 84176 603 8

Editorial: Ilios Publishing, Oxford, UK (www.iliospublishing.com)
Cartography: The Map Studio
Design: Ken Vail Graphic Design, Cambridge, UK
Index and proofreading: Alison Worthington
Originated by The Electronic Page Company, Cwmbran, UK
Printed and bound in China by L-Rex Printing Company Ltd

05 06 07 08 09   10 9 8 7 6 5 4 3 2

CIP data for this publication is available from the British Library

FOR A CATALOGUE OF ALL BOOKS PUBLISHED BY OSPREY MILITARY AND AVIATION
PLEASE CONTACT:

NORTH AMERICA
Osprey Direct, 2427 Bond Street, University Park, IL 60466, USA
E-mail: info@ospreydirectusa.com

ALL OTHER REGIONS
Osprey Direct UK, P.O. Box 140, Wellingborough,
Northants, NN8 2FA, UK
E-mail: info@ospreydirect.co.uk

www.ospreypublishing.com

Glossary

A brief glossary of key terms is provided below. For a full listing,
see Fortress 13: Norman Stone Castles (1) The British Isles
1066–1216.

Ashlar Smooth, flat masonry blocks.
Bailey A courtyard.
Barbican An outwork that protects a gate.
Batter The base of a wall thickened with a sloping front.
Belfry A wooden tower, often mobile, used either to
overlook a wall or to transfer troops on to it.
Berm The space between a wall and ditch.
Brattice Wooden hoarding built out from a battlement to
command the base of a wall.
Buttress Stone support built against a wall to reinforce it.
Corbel A supporting stone bracket.
Counterscarp The outer slope of a ditch.
Crenel The open section of a battlement.
Crenellation Battlement.
Cross-vault A vault in which two barrel vaults intersect.
Curtain A length of wall surrounding a castle enclosure.
Donjon A great tower or keep, but it can also mean an
upper bailey or lord's private area.
Embrasure An internal opening in a wall, sometimes for the
use of archers.
Enceinte The area enclosed by the castle walls.
Loop A narrow opening in a wall that splays out internally,
designed either to admit light or for shooting through.

Artist's note

Readers may care to note that the original paintings from which
the colour plates in this book were prepared are available for
private sale. All reproduction copyright whatsoever is retained
by the Publishers. All enquiries should be addressed to:

Scorpio Gallery, PO Box 475, Hailsham, East Sussex, BN27 2SL, UK

The Publishers regret that they can enter into no correspondence
upon this matter.

Dedication

For Jane, without whom this would not have been possible.

Conversion table

Units of measurement are provided in metric in this volume.

1 centimetre (cm)	0.3937 inches
1 metre (m)	1.0936 yards
1 kilometre (km)	0.6214 miles

Photographic credits

All photographs and line drawings are the author's own unless
otherwise indicated.

Machicolation Battlement brought forward on corbels to
allow soldiers to command the base of a wall.
Merlon The solid section of a battlement.
Moat A ditch, either wet or dry.
Motte An earth mound.
Mural chamber A vaulted chamber formed in the
thickness of a wall.
Mural passage A vaulted passage formed in the thickness
of a wall.
Mural tower A tower set along a curtain wall.
Parapet The outer wall of a wall-walk.
Pilaster A shallow pier built against a wall to buttress it.
Portcullis A lattice made from wood clad in iron, or
occasionally in iron alone, dropped to block a gate.
Postern A small rear door.
Rampart An earthen bank.
Revetted The side of a ditch, bank or motte faced with
wood, stone or brick.
Ring-work A circular or oval earthwork with bank
and ditch.
Scarp The side of a ditch.
Shell keep A motte in which the timber palisade on the
summit is replaced by a stone wall.
Spur A solid, pointed stone reinforcement at the base of a
tower; also, a finger of high ground.
Vault A curved ceiling of stone.
Vice A spiral stair.
Wing-wall A wall descending the slope of a motte.

Contents

Introduction

The Duchy of Normandy was created in 911 by King Charles the Simple of France to accommodate the Scandinavian followers of the Viking leader, Rollo. The latter had struck a deal with the king of the Franks at the treaty of St Clair-sur-Epte, through which Charles hoped to neutralise the threat from one group while at the same time creating a buffer state against further attacks. The new territory, originally part of the Frankish province of Neustria, became known as 'Normandy', the land of the Northmen. As such, the incomers became part of the feudal way of life that was developing in France, in which a lord gave vassals land in return for military service, or kept them in his household. The Normans also assimilated the continental ideas of knighthood and the practice of fighting from horseback instead of primarily on foot, and soon built up a reputation as some of the best cavalry in Western Europe. In addition to feudalism and knighthood, they were introduced to the castle.

Castles were a relatively recent phenomenon. They seem to have arisen in response to the situation in north-western Frankia after the death of Charlemagne (Charles the Great), whose vast empire had also encompassed Germany and parts of northern Italy. As his sons and grandsons squabbled over territories, there was an inevitable breakdown of central government, probably already in evidence due to the problems of ruling such a vast area. Into this came the Vikings, rowing their shallow-draught vessels up the rivers to plunder where opportunity arose. With little central authority, people in threatened areas, notably in north and west France, were thrown back on their own defence. Nobles set themselves up to protect their lands, recruited knights and other soldiers to serve them, and protected their homes with fortifications. The castle, known in written texts as *castrum*, *castellum*, *munitio*, *municipium* or *oppidum*, was also a symbol of authority. The mounted men within could control an area at least 16km around, the distance a horseman could comfortably ride out and back in a day.

These castles were predominantly built of earth and timber, but a number included stone defences. Their expense meant that initially such examples were rare. The new stone towers were not known as 'keeps', since the word was not used in the medieval period (it first appeared in the English language in 1586 in Sidney's *Arcadia*). The more usual word in France was 'donjon', a term derived from the Latin word '*dominium*' (an allusion to lordship), which is still used in the French language today. The term was not only

A reconstructed view of Le Plessis-Grimoult in Normandy, an early form of castle.

4

used to signify these towers but might also denote a motte or the area of a castle that was the lord's preserve. They were also known as 'great towers'.

Written evidence, relating to the great tower at the ducal castle in Rouen built in the mid-10th century by Duke Richard I (942–96), indicates that stone castles soon appeared in Normandy. The same duke is said to have erected a fortified palace at Bayeux, and his successors carried on this trend. In Normandy, castle building other than by the duke always presented a potential threat to central authority, since feudalism was never as controlled in Normandy as it would initially be in England after the Conquest of 1066: the dukes tried to control construction where possible. Duke Richard I, for example, enfeoffed his brother, Raoul, with Ivry. In the first half of the 11th century castles were already being built not only by magnates but also by lesser vassals, though for the latter the cost involved would mean many were of earth and timber. During the century (mainly the first half) some 26 castles were founded between Caen and Falaise, in the area of Le Cinglais. Large numbers of castles were raised during the unsettled times following the death of Robert the Magnificent in 1035, while young Duke William was a minor. Le Plessis-Grimoult had stone defences, and was held not from the duke but from the Bishop of Bayeux until Grimoult de Plessis lost it in 1047 following the battle of Val-ès-Dunes, when William broke rebel power. His youngest son, Henry I, was responsible for much building in the duchy during his time as both duke and king. The vast Angevin empire that the latter's grandson, Henry II, acquired by inheritance and marriage gradually brought many French castles into his orbit whose walls had not been built by Normans: these have largely been passed over in this volume. The death in 1199 of Henry's son, Richard I the Lionheart, finally gave the wily Philip Augustus the opportunity to seize Normandy from King John, which he did in 1204.

At about the time the Normans were conquering England, other Norman adventurers were carving out homes for themselves in southern Italy and Sicily. At first Normans had arrived as mercenaries in about 1017, employed by the Pope as a counter to pressure from the German emperor in the north and the

The late-11th-century donjon at Valmont, with its flat pilaster buttresses, is seen on the right, with the smaller tower butted against its left side and the later château to its left. The machicolated parapet and enlarged windows were added in the 15th century.

The walls of Caen have been altered over the centuries but still retain the essential line of Duke William's castle of 1047. Some of the rectangular towers may be of late-12th-century date.

Byzantines to the east. The Normans gradually spread over southern Italy and founded the territories of Apulia and Calabria. In 1053 a Norman army from Apulia defeated papal forces at the battle of Civitate. Others crossed to Sicily in 1061 and by 1091 had conquered the whole island, which became a kingdom. As in Normandy, the newcomers were keen to assimilate ideas and culture they saw around them. Sicily, a rich mixture of Greek, Arabic and now Norman styles and customs, situated on the Mediterranean trade routes, was a cultivated and fertile kingdom.

Instability lay behind much of the castle building during the early period. The castles were often built on pre-existing Lombard examples and gradually the autonomous nature of the latter was altered as feudal ideas took hold. In the more mountainous regions of Molise in southern-central Italy, however, and in inland regions, the feudal administrative traditions that went with the castle came up against earlier, Roman, forms of organisation that were not to be overlaid. Such areas were new to the Normans. In Molise, the Norman strongholds were more administrative centres for managing the surrounding country. Sometimes villages or markets flourished near new castles, in areas where it was thought commerce would benefit. The rest of the land was poorly inhabited except for small urban enclaves. In more lowland areas such as Apulia and Calabria, feudal notions on similar lines to those in Normandy prevailed. In Apulia small warrior bands, often commanded by Greeks or Lombards, made the initial conquests, and central authority was slow to become established. In Sicily the island was conquered by a single effort, resulting in many small fiefs and a few large autonomous lordships that took a long time to be modified, including comital families who were a source of instability. The large monastic foundations also resisted feudal services, though the latter gradually came to prominence.

Other Normans would sustain the restless tradition these people made famous, a tradition that would carry them on the First Crusade under Bohemond of Taranto to set up the first crusader principality, with Bohemond proclaimed Prince of Antioch in 1100.

Chronology

Normandy

911	Treaty of St Clair-sur-Epte recognises the Duchy of Normandy.
942	Death of Duke William I, Longsword. Accession of Duke Richard I, the Fearless.
996	Death of Duke Richard I, the Fearless. Accession of Duke Richard II.
1026	Death of Richard II. Accession of Duke Richard III.
1027	Death of Duke Richard III. Accession of Duke Robert I, the Magnificent.
1035	Death of Duke Robert I. Accession of Duke William II, the Bastard.
1046	Revolt of western *vicomtes*.
1047	Battle of Val-ès-Dunes.
1049–50	Capture of Brionne.
1051–52	Siege of Domfront and capture of Alençon.
1052–53	Revolt of William, Count of Arques.
1053	Capture of Arques.
1053–54	Franco-Angevin invasion of Normandy.
1054	Battle of Mortemer drives out invaders.
1057	Second invasion of Normandy. Battle of Varaville drives out invaders.
1058	Capture of Thimert by William. Beginning of siege of Thimert by Henry I of France.
1066	Norman Conquest of England and accession of Duke William II as King William I.
1077	First attack on Normandy by Fulk le Rechin of Anjou and siege of La Flèche.
1078	First revolt of Robert, William's eldest son.
1081	Second attack on Normandy by Fulk le Rechin and second siege of La Flèche.
1083	Second revolt of Robert against King William I.
1087	King William I sacks Mantes. Death of King William I. Accession of King William II. Accession of Duke Robert II.
1095	Preaching of First Crusade.
1100	Death of King William II. Accession of King Henry I.
1106	Capture of Duke Robert by King Henry I, who becomes duke.
1134	Death of Duke Robert II.
1135	Death of King Henry I. Accession of King Stephen.
1144	Geoffrey of Anjou conquers Normandy during civil war.
1154	Death of King Stephen. Accession of King Henry II.
1173–74	Revolt of Henry's sons, and attacks of Louis VII of France.
1188–89	Second revolt of sons of King Henry II.
1189	Death of King Henry II. Accession of King Richard I.
1190	King Richard leads the Third Crusade to the Holy Land.

The so-called Exchequer Hall in Caen castle was damaged in 1944, but restored. It is one of the earliest and finest secular halls in Normandy.

1192–94	Philip II captures Norman border castles.
1194–98	Recapture of fortresses by Richard.
1199	Death of King Richard I. Accession of King John.
1203–04	Siege of Château-Gaillard.
1204	Loss of Normandy.

Southern Italy and Sicily

1017	Norman mercenaries arrive in Italy.
1053	Battle of Civitate (near present-day San Paolo di Civitate, *prov.* Foggia).
1058–62	Siege of citadel at Capua.
1061	Norman Conquest of Sicily begins.
1068–71	Siege of Bari.
1071–72	Siege of Palermo.
	Roger I is made Great Count of Sicily.
1073	Siege of Amalfi.
1076–77	Siege of Salerno.
1081	Robert Guiscard invades Byzantine Empire. Guiscard and Bohemond take Corfu.
1081	Sea battle off Durazzo (Dyrrachium).
1081–82	Siege of Durazzo (Dyrrachium).
1082	Normans capture Damascus.
1085	Death of Robert Guiscard.
1090	Normans capture Malta and Gozo.
1091	Norman Conquest of Sicily completed.
1100	Bohemond of Taranto is proclaimed Prince of Antioch.
1101	Death of Roger I of Sicily.
1107–08	Siege of Durazzo (Dyrrachium) by Bohemond. A treaty is forced on him and he leaves for Italy.
1111	Death of Bohemond of Taranto.
1130	Election of Roger d'Hauteville as King Roger II of Sicily.
c.1134	Normans invade Tunisia.
1154	Death of Roger II of Sicily. Accession of William I, the Bad.
1166	Death of William the Bad. Accession of William II, the Good.
1184	Papal forces capture Rome supported by Guiscard.
1189	Death of William the Good of Sicily.
1190	Accession of Tancred of Lecce.
1194	Death of Tancred. Accession and death of William III.

The walls of Caen.

Design and development

Normandy

In Normandy the duke was technically in charge of all castle building, but in practice some lords put up their own defences: allodial land (which the family alone owned) existed here too. Some castles were the direct responsibility of the ruler: Henry I of England in particular pursued a programme of adding strong stone fortifications to a number of sites as Duke of Normandy. When the Norman duchy expanded, notably under Henry II, many other castles came under the Norman/Angevin umbrella. Some, such as the huge donjon at Loches, were pre-existing stone fortresses in many ways similar to Norman examples but constructed previously by workmen from other duchies or counties.

Castle building in Normandy has an earlier history than it does in England. The first castles erected in Normandy were mainly of earth and timber, for economic reasons. The simplest form was what we now call a 'ringwork', consisting of a courtyard protected by a ditch, the earth from which formed a bank on the inner side, topped by a palisade (a row of stakes). However, some castles were already using stone for the walls or had replaced timber with stone. Longueville-sur-Scie was first built for the Giffard family in the 11th century at the bottom of the Scie valley near the town, and is in the form of a vast oval delimited by earthen walls, with no motte (a mound of earth). The castle was rebuilt in the late-11th to early-12th century on top of a hill on the site of Saint-Foy priory, as a large oval enceinte with walls but no mural towers. A wall of the gate-tower (mentioned in texts as a large tower at the entrance, facing the plateau) survives behind a facing wall, but there is no trace of a donjon. When the castle of Le Plessis-Grimoult was abandoned in 1047, it consisted of a 4m-high earthen rampart topped with a stone wall with one or more mural towers and a stone gatehouse.

William the Conqueror's move to make Caen his new centre saw the construction of an impressive castle on a rocky outcrop in about 1060, covering 12.5 acres. The long curtain wall initially lacked mural towers, but was provided with some rectangular mural towers probably in the late-12th century. Their irregular and wide spacing, with consequent loss of effective defence, belies the residential layout of the original castle.

The motte first appeared as an element in castle design during the 11th century. Sometimes natural but usually artificial, it was set at the side of the courtyard or sometimes within it, forming what

The donjon at Domfront was probably built by Henry I in the early-12th century. The first-floor entrance can be seen on the right.

9

Only two walls of the donjon at Domfront survive, but they stand above the rest of the fortifications in the foreground, which form part of the defended gate and possibly date from 1202–03.

A plan view of the western walls of Domfront, with the polygonal twin gate towers perhaps built by John in 1202–03.

is now termed a motte and bailey castle. At Maulévrier-Sainte-Gertrude there is additionally an arc-shaped outer bailey whose walls cross the ditch at each end to join those of the inner bailey. The puissant shape of the motte emphasised the nature of lordship, and the summit also allowed a better view, often being crowned by a palisade enclosing a wooden tower. The palisade might be replaced with stone, forming a shell keep, sometimes with buildings. For example, between 1120 and 1130 a polygonal wall was built round the motte at Vatteville-la-Rue, with buttresses. Similarly at Gisors, the Conqueror's son, Henry I, built a wall around the top of the motte in the second quarter of the 12th century, a polygonal structure of 22 facets, each corner covered by a flat pilaster buttress, with three turrets on the north side. Hacqueville is one of the best-preserved examples in Normandy. The mound is some 53m in diameter at the summit, with a 12th-century wall, the remains of which are included in the present farmhouse. On the summit, a square cellar with four rooms was reached by a right-angled stair lit by a basement window. Sometimes, as at Château-sur-Epte, the stone walls followed the side of the motte down to connect with those around the bailey. Occasionally a stone tower was raised on the motte, though this was a difficult procedure. Most artificial mounds, despite being made from layers of rammed earth, were not sufficiently settled to withstand the weight of a stone tower on top, unless it sat on the natural ground level and the motte covered the lower stages. The castle of La Haye-du-Puits is now ruined, but the huge motte on which the main stone castle stands is well preserved. The site originally featured an earth and timber castle, but probably in the 12th century (perhaps the first quarter) the palisade on the motte was replaced by a circular or polygonal stone wall; added to this was a slender, quadrangular stone donjon of three stages, which probably replaced a timber tower.

At this time, stone was already being used in north-west France to construct large square or rectangular buildings. The earliest survivors are not Norman, but located further south, in the area of the Loire. The famous castles of Doué-la-Fontaine and Langeais represent perhaps the first stone buildings still visible. Doué-la-Fontaine has been dated to about 950: it was built to serve as a ground-floor hall, but was altered to a tower with a first-floor entrance after a fire. Langeais was built perhaps in 994 or 1017; it too may have been a castle hall rather than a tower. The stone hall at Brionne that was attacked by Duke William doubled as a donjon. Stone curtain walls would always hold the advantage over those of timber because they were fireproof, but initially some stone buildings

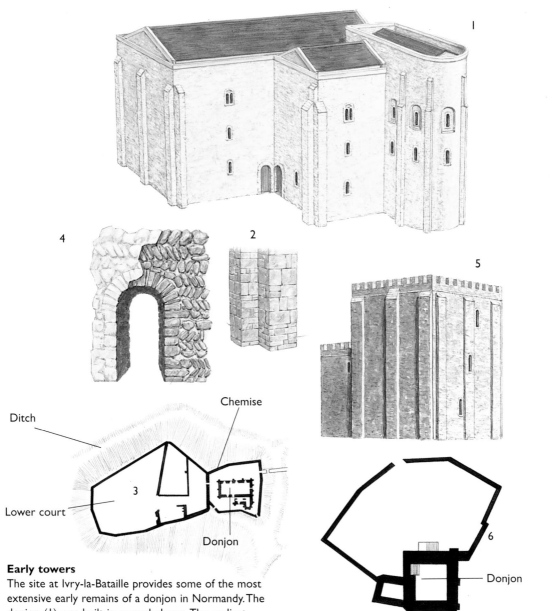

Ditch

Chemise

Lower court

Donjon

Donjon

Early towers

The site at Ivry-la-Bataille provides some of the most extensive early remains of a donjon in Normandy. The donjon (1) was built in several phases. The earliest form, dating probably from the early-11th century, is tentatively reconstructed here. The tower (32m x 25m) may have been a storey lower, but the fact that Orderic Vitalis refers to it as the 'famous tower' even in the 12th century suggests it was of suitable stature. The absence of ashlar and the square buttresses (2) are symbolic of its early date. The apsidal end is that of the chapel within, and there was one main large room and a smaller at the side. Perhaps due to a change of plan or later demolition or collapse, the smaller room was extended to form a second wall, the original outer wall now becoming a spine wall dividing the larger and smaller rooms. A similar design, even to a similar apse,

was to be seen again in the White Tower begun by William the Conqueror in London in about 1076. The tower is set within a chemise wall that seems to have been built at the same time or possibly earlier, and which is connected to a lower court, as shown in the plan view (3). The later towers have been removed from the plan. Also shown is an external doorway seen from the inside of the great tower (4). The rather plain tower at Valmont (5), dating from about 1100, is seen here without the later crenellated battlements. It forms the nucleus of the castle, whose basic enclosure is shown in the accompanying plan (6).

The remains of the chapel of Saint-Symphorien, dating from the 11th or 12th century. The priory was situated within the enceinte of Domfront.

may have been erected with defence as only a secondary consideration.

It is by no means clear exactly what function the earliest stone towers were designed to fulfil. Some of them were cramped and lacking in charm, while others would have provided comfortable accommodation. It would be dangerous to label all donjons as performing a similar role. Some of the larger examples may have been designed primarily as statements of power, to be employed for important functions rather than everyday use. The expense involved in erecting such a building would, of course, be enormous, but it would imply that its owner was a man of vision and substance. Used for official receptions, its impact on visitors perhaps familiar only with wooden secular buildings would be notable. Some others may have been designed both for receptions and as a withdrawing area for the lord and his family. Some smaller donjons perhaps served as a solar tower, an adjunct perhaps to a timber great hall that has now vanished. The smallest towers are difficult to relate to any domestic purpose because of their cramped interiors: it should be remembered that even a lord and his immediate family would have servants to hand, who might sleep in the same room. Perhaps such small towers served mainly as military watchtowers, while still displaying wealth and power in their construction materials.

While impressive remains and donjons survive in many places cited in documents, most of these donjons were erected in the 12th century and do not accurately represent a castle when first built. They may have replaced initial timber structures, or were a new addition to the castle. Unfortunately, very few stone towers survive from the early period in Normandy. The remains of the tower at Ivry-la-Bataille date to around 1000: the architect is said to have been beheaded by Aubrey, wife of the holder, Count Raoul d'Ivry, to prevent him building for anyone else. Others that were raised in the early period (though not necessarily in stone to begin with) include Tillières, Falaise, Le Homme (the present l'Isle Marie), Cherbourg and Brix, under Richard II (996–1026) and Richard III (1026–27); and Cherrueix (and perhaps others) under Robert I, the Magnificent (1027–35).

In his account of Duke William II's attack on the castle of Brionne in 1047, William of Poitiers describes it as having a stone hall 'serving the defenders as a donjon (*arx*)'. At Avranches, detailed study of what little remains has led both Impey and Nicolas-Méry to suggest a construction date of between 1000 and 1040: the tower must have been impressive, covering an area of 37m × 27m. The square tower at Valmont is another early example, probably from the 11th century, though it now forms part of a much later overbuild. The castle remains, however, a simple enclosure with the donjon at one side. The building itself is an unfussy square tower, with walls 2.4m thick and about 22m high, with a single room on each floor: it may have been a solar tower for a vanished hall. It has three buttresses along three sides (those by the corners do not join to clasp them), which supported a primitive wooden gallery.

Orderic Vitalis

Orderic was the son of a Norman father and an English mother. As a boy he was sent from England to the monastery of Saint-Évroul in the southern borderlands of Normandy, where he lived as a monk and was brought up with sons of the knightly class. His great work, *The Ecclesiastical History*, written between 1114 and 1141, includes numerous references to contemporary siege warfare and castles. Orderic gleaned much of this from conversations with royal household knights and members of neighbouring families, plus those of benefactors and magnates. Many references are to military movements in this turbulent area, lending an authority and immediacy to the stories.

The tower at Ivry-la-Bataille has led some to speculate that it may have been the prototype for the earliest Norman donjons erected in England, namely those at the Tower of London and Colchester: both of these have an internal cross-wall and an apsidal corner marking the chapel. Moreover, although Ivry-la-Bataille was by then several decades old, it must have held some status, since Orderic Vitalis (see p.12), writing in the first half of the 12th century, refers to it as the 'famous tower'. There must also have been some fortification at Rouen in the early period, since it was the first city of Normandy and would remain so even after Duke William shifted his power base westward to Caen. Some form of tower can be seen on the Bayeux Tapestry (probably worked within 20 years of the Conquest in 1066) but exactly what it looked like can only be speculation, as it was completely destroyed.

Rufus's brother, Henry I (1106–35), undertook a programme of building leading to the appearance of extant donjons in a number of castles. Most of the donjons are square or rectangular, have internal cross-walls, pilaster buttresses and first-floor entrances. Some of these forms are similar to towers built by Henry in England. As Duke of Normandy, Henry had already been busy at Domfront: the Bellême family had built a fortress there in the first quarter of the 11th century, before Henry erected his donjon (after 1092 and before 1123). Henry made Domfront his main base in Normandy. The castle sits on the end of an outcrop, dominating the Varenne valley, and is cut off from the town by a deep ditch. In the 12th century the town was surrounded by a wall with 24 towers, remains of which are still visible. Only two walls of the donjon remain, about 28m high and 3m thick, with four or perhaps five floors. It was one of the largest towers in Normandy, with a total external area of 26.3m × 22.4m, and an internal one of 20.3m × 16.4m. The corners were clasped by granite buttresses with a further buttress in the centre face of each wall. Internally, the space was divided by a cross-wall and further subdivided by another at right angles on one side. Neither the ground-floor nor third-floor walls have any loops at all. The entrance was on the first floor of the western wall via a gate in a vaulted arch some 6m above ground. There may have been a cistern in the north-west angle and also cellars separated by walls. Flooring was supported on beams running into holes. The donjon became a model for Henry's later work as Duke and King, such as at Caen, Arques and Falaise.

Falaise features a rectangular buttressed donjon (the *Grand Donjon*) in the north-west corner of the site, overlooking a cliff and a stream running below. The south-east corner was expanded to form the St Pritz Chapel, with a small newel stair. The ground floor is blind (i.e. without loops for light) and the first floor is the only other level to survive. Access to the donjon was by a straight stair up to the first floor on the east side, with the main newel in the north-east corner. During the mid-12th century a second, smaller, rectangular tower (the *Petit Donjon*) was attached to the west side of the *Grand Donjon*, with access through the wall. It had a small room block jutting north along the west face.

Henry I largely rebuilt Arques-la-Bataille. The castle consisted of a generous bailey with deep ditches, opening on to the plateau on the south. The curtain walls have been rebuilt and ruined over the centuries, but there are two square mural towers along the south face, and a possible third, that may be of the period of Henry I. The rest are D-shaped 13th-century structures, and there are later gatehouses. The French *doyen* of reconstruction, Viollet-le-Duc, studied the ruined castle in conjunction with a plan of 1708, and reconstructed both the castle site and the donjon, making the latter conform to how he thought it once appeared. Henry's donjon is now in a ruinous state: it was some 20m square and about 20m high, positioned at an angle close to the curtain in the north-west corner of the inner bailey, where it also guarded the postern gate. It had an internal cross-wall, main stairwell in the south corner, and the south-eastern face was provided with two large buttresses. The external straight stair was enclosed in a large forebuilding accessible by a doorway on the

Henry I's donjon at Falaise is perched at one end of the castle on the rock overlooking the stream. Legend says Arletta was bathing at this spot when Duke Robert spied her from his castle; William the Conqueror was the issue of their union. The Grand Donjon (of about 1120) stands to the left of the Petit Donjon, while the cylindrical tower of Philip Augustus was added in about 1200.

south-east face and opened onto the second floor. The lowest floor was vaulted throughout. Viollet-le-Duc interpreted the buttresses as connecting at second-floor level by semi-circular arches. A mural dead-end passageway on the fourth (top) floor ran from the stair newel along the south-east side, and contained two pairs of lights that opened into it, suggesting arrow loops, though there is no embrasure inside the passage. Another passage ran back via an extension to the north-west curtain wall.

In 1123 Henry I rebuilt the small donjon at Vire, which would become a key residence of King John. The first courtyard was backed up by a second behind it, in which there was a chapel to Saint Blaise: at the rear the donjon rose up. Only the west wall and half the south wall survive to any extent. The donjon measures externally 14m × 13.4m and 9.6m × 9.2m internally. The destroyed north wall was some 2.3m thick, while that on the south is 2.1m thick. The external angles are clasped by flat buttresses that project 0.3m. The walls are of sandstone; internally the donjon was divided into two unequal rooms by a north-south partition wall. There are four floors (the ground floor without openings), with the first floor higher than the others. On the top floor the surviving west wall has a row of corbels to carry the floor beams that presumably ran to those of the vanished cross-wall. On the ground floor there is a simple narrow window embrasure. The two main floors seem to be the first and second floors, with the first floor served by a fireplace and a window converted later in the Middle Ages. On the second floor two windows open on the west wall (Chatelain noted there should be one in the middle of the south wall), and on the third floor the windows are very narrow, which has been

The interior of the donjon at Falaise during renovation, and prior to the insertion of new floors. The top floor with its two light windows can be clearly seen.

attributed to the fact that the garrison who guarded the battlement were located here. The crenellations were replaced in the 14th-century by machicolations.

Not all donjons were built by the Anglo-Norman kings of course. At Brionne the tower has been attributed to Robert I of Meulan in the early-12th century to replace an earlier castle on an islet in the River Risle in the town, which had been besieged in 1047 and 1090. The donjon has one and a half walls surviving to a height of about 17m but originally was 20m square, its walls 4m thick and supported by buttresses. It consisted of three floors, the lowest being blind; the first floor had windows. The donjon appears to have been partially rebuilt, perhaps in the second half of the 12th century, as a fireplace is blocked by 12th-century rubble. On the top floor traces of a single roof gable are visible on the interior wall face. A row of quadrangular

The blind basement and the first floor of the donjon at Falaise.

holes along the upper part of the northern wall was probably for wooden hoardings. Tancarville was the seat of the Chamberlains of Normandy from about 1100. There is a 12th-century square residential tower (the *Tour-carrée*) at the north-west angle. The donjon built by William de Mandeville at Chambois (measuring 21.4m × 15.4m externally, with a height of 25.7m) dates from the second half of the 12th century and is the best preserved in Normandy. It was built using small blocks, with four turrets rising in limestone freestone. It has a windowless ground floor and two floors above, pierced by geminate (two-light) windows. The entrance on the first floor was reached via a small forebuilding on the south-eastern side. Each floor has a large chimney, and each corner houses a mural chamber.

During the 12th century cylindrical or polygonal donjons began to appear, which benefited from an absence of weak corners and blind spots. Gisors was provided with an irregular eight-sided polygonal donjon on the motte by Henry I, about 20m high and of four stages. Between 1170 and 1180 Henry II

Falaise castle seen from the courtyard, showing the donjon's first-floor entrance, now masked by a modern forebuilding. Philip's tower is clearly visible.

raised the donjon by two storeys and added five buttresses to reinforce it. At Bricquebec a polygonal donjon sits on the motte but whether it is partly 12th century or wholly 14th century is unclear. Mortemer has a buttressed cylindrical donjon built by a half-brother of Henry II in the late-1100s on similar lines to Orford in England. Richard I built a circular donjon at Bonneville-sur-Touques at the end of the 12th century. Conches-en-Ouche was built around the same time on an escarpment at the junction of ducal lands and those of the Tosny family. The cylindrical donjon, closely surrounded by its enclosure, is set on a partly man-made motte and cut off from the plateau by ditches

A view of the castle of Falaise, showing the curtain wall of the bailey with its towers, many of which are of 13th-century date.

10m deep and 20m wide. It has a main hall vaulted with ogival (pointed) arches. The walls are 2.6m thick and are pierced by six openings. There are stairs in the thickness of the wall as well as a rising shaft up to the main hall. At Neaufles-Saint-Martin the motte carries the remains of a cylindrical donjon built in the 1180s by Henry II, 20m high and 14m in diameter, with three floors on corbels, the top floor with bonded oculi (circular openings). La Roche-Guyon has a late-12th-century donjon *en bec* (literally, 'in beak'), with one side drawn out to a solid stone vertical edge, to deflect missiles and present a solid obstacle to siege engines. Château-sur-Epte, founded in 1087 by William Rufus, has a bailey of some 70m and a motte of 50m diameter at ground level: at the top is a very dilapidated circular tower probably added by Henry II in 1184, which is surrounded by a wall pierced (probably later) with loops.

A number of towns, especially those that grew next to castles or had a castle planted in proximity, were given curtain walls and mural towers, though often surviving examples date from the 13th century. The town that grew at the foot of Falaise castle had a dressed wooden palisade at the end of the 10th century, which was replaced by a stone wall under Richard II. This was repaired by both Duke Robert the Magnificent and William the Conqueror, but a new wall was built by Henry I in c.1123. Repaired over the centuries, the wall eventually had about 50 towers and six gates, and ran for approximately two kilometres.

Southern Italy

In southern Italy (and Sicily) the Norman adventurers saw to their own defences, largely adding to existing Byzantine, Lombard or Arab structures as they saw fit. Local craftsmen must have been employed in these endeavours. In some instances the latters' influence on the final design is tangible.

The earliest Norman strongholds in Italy were the hill fortresses of Aversa (given to Rannulf by Segius IV in 1030 for services, who subsequently became Count of Aversa and was perhaps the first to give up brigandage) and Melfi (already a hilltop stronghold that had been heavily fortified by the Greeks). In 1044 Gaimar the Iron Hand opened up the mountainous and rather desolate region of Calabria, and built the important fortress of Squillace. Between 1050 and 1060 Aversa expanded to become the Norman principality of Capua (1057) and Melfi the duchy of Apulia. In 1056, Robert Guiscard (later Duke of Apulia and Calabria, and the founder of the Norman state of the Two Sicilies) placed his recently arrived younger brother Roger (later Count of Sicily) in Mileto. Molise County, roughly present-day Isernia, came into being in 1055, and Loritello County in 1061 (the eastern part of the modern-day Molise region).

We know that prior to 1055 Robert Guiscard had begun building strongholds in Calabria, such as at the old Byzantine fortress of Rossano on the Ionian coast (which came under William of Grantmesnil and was the centre of his honour), and 'Scribla', a hot and potentially malarial fortress guarding a mountain pass in the Val di Crati, and San Marco Argentano in the area of Cosenza. Also in this area lay Scalea, which was built in 1058 and looked down on the sea from on high.

Of particular note among the castles built in Apulia are Mount Sant'Angelo, whose pentagonal Tower of Giants was erected by Guiscard; Castelpagano, run by the Norman count Henry; and the castles to the south of the River Fortore such as Dragonara and Fiorentino (built by the Catepano Bojannes), Bovino (built by the Norman Dragone or perhaps by the counts of Lorotello, on Roman remains), Deliceto (erected in 1073 by the Norman Tristainus) and Serracapriola (dating beyond the Normans to the 9th century). Additionally, fortified convents were to be found at San Marco la Catola, San Marco in Lamis, Ripalta, and Calena.

Many surviving castles were modified at a later date, such as the Langobard town fortress of Roccapipirozzi, and few original examples remain. Early castles were often (though not always) built of wood, increasingly supplemented by, or wholly in, stone. Typical features include an inner courtyard, and a first-floor entrance: often, later additions were made such as reinforcements to walls, or domestic buildings, which altered the walls of the enceinte. At Conversano, 18km from Monopoli, the castle is trapezoid and three of the 12th-century square towers survive, together with a cylindrical 14th-century example. Towers, such as Morrone, were usually built along river courses, often on mid-slope within sight of each other and of a town.

In the early Norman period existing city walls and defences were utilised by the incoming Normans. Where ecclesiastical and military powers enjoyed good relationships, church, castle and residential buildings stood together and town squares were formed. Vastogirardi was a fortified burgh of an irregular shape with thick walls surrounding an open courtyard, and buildings attached around the inner sides with vaulted ground floors: it provided a solid defensive structure with two entrances diametrically opposed.

In more mountainous regions the town would spread along the ridge, with the church still the focal point. Town walls would evolve and the castle might find itself in the role of citadel, the place of final defence. Later castles were often built on the edge of an existing town, such as Venafro on the hill of Sant'Angelo. At Fornelli the Normans appear to have improved existing structures by integrating curtain wall sections and reorganising towers: it was later heavily rebuilt. Longano and the Oratino make use of rocky ridges with escarpments, with Oratino including Norman work in its four-sided tower. Such towers were sometimes used as mural or corner towers, with dressed corners, as at Cercepiccola and Gambatesa. The latter is set on a ridge overlooking the confluence of the River Fortore and the Tappino stream. First mentioned in the mid-12th century, it is a four-sided structure with inner courtyard and two square corner towers, but the walls have been much altered.

Naturally strong hill or mountain areas abound in Molise province, making for excellent strongholds such as Mount Ferrante and Mount Santa Croce. Such places might be of Samnitic origin, reused by the Romans, and the Normans named them *castellum vetus* ('old fortress'). Old walled burghs were reused, but additional fortresses were built in the Norman period and later. Polygonally cut local stone was used, or else large rough-cut stone set in irregular rows. Castle walls built on rocky outcrops or along hill crests might have their foundations set in carved terraces, such as at Pescolanciano, known in the time of William II and with a trapezoid floor plan. Castel Bagnoli del Trigno was a Langobard castle on a rocky spur overlooking the Trigno river valley. The Normans modified the existing fortifications, building escarped walls, slightly pronounced, and overhanging on three sides. The front entrance wall is more prominent. Castropignano castle (another Langobard fortress) sits on a rocky ridge cut off from the town by a ditch (now filled in): it too was rebuilt by the Normans. It consisted of a four-sided castle with donjon and towers, including an entrance tower and one overlooking the River Biferno. The curtain wall displays a variety of building techniques, using calcareous stone set in regular pattern, and overhangs the rock, which is sometimes cut into terraces or escarpments. The gatehouse has a guardroom with two long arrow loops.

In some cases (for example at Roccamandolfi, on a hilltop overlooking the Matese pass) platforms and ramps were created by shovelling earth and protecting them with straight walls. The tops of outcrops or long ridges were adapted and surrounded by curtain walls sometimes set with mural towers and bayonet entrances, by spurs, 'rompitratta' walls, or (rarely) 'caisson' structures. At Roccamandolfi, the enceinte follows the irregular hillside and incorporates a four-sided structure, possibly a donjon. Cylindrical and D-shaped towers were added, while on one side the walls are integrated almost with the rock: on the southern side holes for horizontal wooden beams added within the masonry show construction techniques. This work is known as *opus gallicum* ('Gallic work', based on an ancient technique), and Molisian examples reflect the swift construction necessary. In the Magliano tower in the town of Santa Croce timber beams form a double mesh of bars radial to the masonry. Another example is Riporse Castle in Longano, where a four-sided enceinte rests on an earthen mound, possibly a motte. Inside are the ruins of a square tower and cistern, with two out of four D-shaped mural towers remaining. Regular rows of small stones with much mortar is evident. Another example is the ruins of Castellerci at Palata.

In the lowlands the standard form of castle was the *castrum*, usually on the outskirts of towns or villages: these were initially strongholds for troops. The earliest examples were first Scribla, built by Guiscard, and later San Marco in Calabria. The *quadriburgium* was a four-sided building with corner towers: many have been overbuilt so as to incorporate the Norman castle, for example the palace at Larino. The term *castellum* could mean a strongpoint outside a settlement, a *castrum* or a light structure placed against a besieged gate, or later a citadel built within a burgh.

Donjons, square and later cylindrical, were built, but were also copied by later builders. The donjon at San Marco Argentano in Calabria was built by Guiscard in 1051. At Campobasso, the donjon was erected by the Normans on the site of a Lombard tower with remains of Samnite walls beneath: it was situated in a four-sided castle, with four circular corner towers added later. Riccia castle, on the eastern side of two hills and overlooking the valley formed between them, was built on an ancient site and has an enceinte with three circular towers and a cylindrical donjon comprising a basement and three stories. The master tower of the 'sea' castle at Palermo, documented in the 12th century, is a cylindrical tower with spur, as is the late-Norman donjon at Bovino. Donjons were placed either well within the defences or in the most prominent position. In Molise they are almost always on the edge of an old town, usually isolated from the walls.

Sicily

The brothers Roger and Robert Guiscard executed a similar plan of castle building in Sicily. In 1060 Roger launched an abortive attack on Messina but captured it after a second invasion. Robert spent a week reinforcing and extending the walls and towers, raising ramparts and throwing up earthworks; a cavalry garrison was installed. Following the wishes of the local Greek Christians, Robert built the first Norman castle in Sicily in 1060–61 at San Marco d'Alunsio in the Val Demone, near the classical Aluntium: the ruins still survive. Petralia Soprana near Cefalù soon followed. From about 1062 Roger

The Norman invasion of Sicily

Prior to the Norman invasion, Sicily was ruled by three emirs, who competed with one another. In 1060 and 1061 Roger crossed the Straits of Messina to make abortive attacks on the city: when Robert arrived too the city fell. The next year Roger was back and settled in Troina. However it was not until 1071 that the Normans moved effectively; Robert Guiscard and Roger occupied Catania, then moved by land (Roger) and sea (Robert) against Palermo. The latter, an extremely rich city, fell in 1072. The Norman hold on the island, mainly of the north, was still uncertain though, and castles had probably appeared at Calascibetta, Mazzara and Paternò by 1074. A major opponent, Ibn-el-Werd, emir of Syracuse, blocked Roger for a decade, but in 1085 Norman ships and land forces besieged and took the city. In 1087 Enna fell too. In 1090 Malta and Gozo were seized and by 1091 Roger, the 'Great Count', ruled Sicily. His son, Roger II (crowned king of Sicily in 1130), would rule Sicily and southern Italy, and would defeat a German imperial expedition to Italy in 1136–37. King Roger's son, William I (the Bad) acceded in 1154, and his son, William II (the Good), ruled from 1166 until 1189. The following year the latter's illegitimate cousin, Tancred of Lecce, took over, but both he and his son, William III, died in 1194. The Emperor Henry VI finally took Sicily in 1194–95.

Norman Sicily

When the Normans arrived in Italy and spread across to Sicily, they tended at first to build defences similar to those in their homeland. Hence the rather plain tower of Adrano in Sicily (1) is divided by a cross-wall and subordinate walls to form hall, chamber and chapel (shown in the plan view, 1a). By the late-12th century the Normans had become much more immersed in the surrounding Lombard, Byzantine and Muslim styles. The main illustration (2) shows the palace tower of La Ziza in Palermo, at the time of building (1162) set in gardens among fruit trees and pools. The grand entrance leads into a large central room rising through the floor above to a honeycombed ceiling, with a frieze running in and out of wall niches. In front of the palace stands a covered fountain with water channels running into the main tower. A plan view of La Ziza is also shown (2a). La Cuba (3), also in Palermo, likewise shows strong influence from Islamic art and architecture. Built around 1180, it was set within a lake in the royal park and had a first-floor entrance.

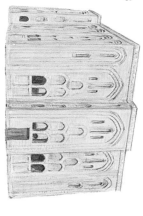

2a

2

3

1

1a

The interior of the donjon at Vire. The fireplace on the right has lost its stone hood.

A plan of Vire.

made Troina, perched on its hilltop, his centre of operations for several years. Between 1071 and 1074, following the capture of Palermo, he endeavoured to consolidate his hold over northern Sicily. He built a castle at Mazara in 1073, whose ruins survive; and one at Paternò the same year (the ruins have been heavily restored). Further castles were located at Calascibetta, Trapani, Lentini, Termini and Milazzo. In 1087 Roger Borsa rebuilt the fortifications of Agrigento, and Enna finally passed to the Normans by agreement with its ruler, Ibn Hamud, who retired to Calabria. Much of this work involved restoring walls and adding new stonework or towers to existing ones. Some fortresses had proved to be quite effectively protected, as the Normans discovered.

A solitary Norman tower of the castle at Caltabellotta survives on its heights, overlooking the *Chiesa Madre*. Adrano (or Aderno) has a large rectangular tower that lacks buttresses of any kind. The first-floor entrance is reached by a straight stair along the outer wall. Provided with two barrel vaults, it is divided internally into two separate rooms, one of which is further subdivided. There is a chapel on the second floor. The stair vice is set in the centre of one wall rather than at the corner. The surrounding chemise with small round corner towers is probably late-13th-century work.

Two notable palace towers survive in Palermo. La Ziza (from the Arabic word *aziz*, meaning 'magnificent') is the best preserved, and was begun by William I 'The Bad' (king of Sicily 1154–66) in 1162: it was finished off by his son, William II 'The Good' (king of Sicily 1166–89). A tall, two-storey rectangular building heavily influenced by Arab decoration, it has rooms set round a principal, central room that rises through them. La Cuba, also in Palermo, was built by William II. Set in an ornamental lake within the royal park (alas, no longer), it has a first-floor entrance, though much of the fabric has now been destroyed. Nearby are the remains of a smaller, second building, the Cubula, and not far off the remnants of arcading (on the east front of the Villa Napoli) that mark the site of the small Cuba Soprana (a pre-Norman palace).

The costs of construction

As previously noted, stone was an expensive commodity, and transporting it was as expensive as the cost of the stone itself. One study has estimated that moving stone 18km doubled its quarried price. Sometimes nearby stone quarries were utilised, or local stone if it was of good enough quality, especially for rubble infill. The building of the castles of Caen, Falaise and Château-Gaillard, for example, all employed this means of keeping costs down. The early castle at Ivry-la-Bataille used local tufa limestone mixed with banks of flint in a herringbone pattern. Several quarries were situated in the very interior of the enceinte wall of Caen castle, under the site of the current Musée des Beaux-Arts. These quarries were either subterranean or else open air, and recently others have been found during work on an underground car park. Some stone, however, had to be brought from further afield: Bretteville is one early quarry site mentioned in 11th-century sources. The overall cost of constructing a castle varied between sites, depending on the amount of work involved. For the building of the great castle of Château-Gaillard, Richard I spent about £11,500. During his time the government of Normandy was responsible for the upkeep of about 45 castles.

In southern Italy, during the 12th century a guild of stonemasons was established at Santa Maria di Guglieto, in Molise. Here, especially in an unstable area, a fortification might be built using local stone quarries or material found on an existing monument site. For this reason the quality of work was not always of the highest standard. Walls were often built of rough-cut masonry, sometimes scabbled, and even the use of dressed stone edges and decorative elements was not common. A peculiar feature of castles built here is the way walls taper off towards the top, with corbels used for supporting floor beams. The ground floor was often vaulted in stone too, and together with the basement this housed the storerooms and cistern. (Further details of the techniques and methods of construction can be found in Fortress 13: *Norman Stone Castles (1) The British Isles 1066–1216*.)

Henry I's donjon at Vire, built around 1123, survives as two walls. The rock base can be seen.

Tour of a castle: Château-Gaillard

Château-Gaillard (or 'Roche d'Andeli', to use its official name) was built by Richard I of England on the banks of the River Seine in the Norman Vexin, the disputed territory claimed by both the Norman dukes and the French kings. In the valley of the Andelle, Richard decided to block further incursions by the French King Philip in 1194, and so he built Radepont as a new line of defence on the river. There may have been a castle here in the time of Henry I, but the existing fortress is the work of Richard I, along with Moulineaux, Orival. He then turned his attention to the two Andelys, Grand and Petit Andely. The River Gambon flows into the Seine from the north, and at the confluence is an island on which the little town of Petit Andely was set out: to the west of it lies a further, smaller island, the Ile d'Andely. To the north-east, on the far bank of the Gambon, lay Grand Andely. Both towns were fortified by Richard, with walls and towers; one of the latter remains on the west of Grand Andely. Two bridges crossed the Gambon to connect the towns with the Ile d'Andely, which was also walled. Close to Petit Andely, rising above the Seine, is a chalk spur that overlooks the little town, and it was here that the king chose to site his new castle. Its position on the Seine would command river traffic moving both north towards the Norman capital of Rouen, and south towards Paris. Construction of the castle was swift: begun in 1196, it was completed in an amazing 13 months. Richard is said to have remarked, 'How beautiful is my one-year old daughter'. The size of the project makes it all the more impressive. Richard called his new castle 'Gaillard', usually interpreted as 'saucy', though it can also mean 'bold' or 'strong'. He swore that it was so good that he would hold it if it were made of butter. However, the king died in 1199, and it was left to his younger brother, John, to uphold the boast.

A view of Château-Gaillard from the east, with the River Seine behind. The donjon can be seen on the right. On the left the outer bailey with its triangular curtain is cut off from the main castle by a deep ditch.

The site for the new castle was well chosen: the steep, sloping rock face meant that a hostile army's only practical approach was from the south-east. This was enhanced by the digging of a deep ditch around the landward side to the north and east.

Richard had envisaged a castle with several courtyards. At the south-eastern end he constructed the outer courtyard, the first obstacle for an attacker. The top of the ridge here was provided with a circuit of walls, roughly triangular in plan, with the apex facing south-east and covered by a large circular tower, with two further towers behind. It is assumed that another tower lay at the south-west angle, though the walls here have now been destroyed. The third angle to the north-east hosted the entrance itself: it comprised a rectangular gate-tower flanked on one side by a D-shaped tower (this does not survive). A gate passage flanked by two towers (as built at Dover by Richard's father, Henry II) was not employed, despite the use of modern cylindrical towers at Château-Gaillard. The outer courtyard was cut off from the rest of the castle by a ditch cut through the solid rock. Access to the second, middle courtyard was via a bridge over the ditch but only fragments of the entrance gate of the middle bailey have survived. The gate may have been through a central opening in the wall or possibly more to the north-east end, but either way does not appear to have been heavily defended. The bridge itself seems to have been a dog-leg shape in order to line up both gates. The middle courtyard was also protected by a curtain wall that ran in a rather angular oval around the rest of

The deep ditches of Château-Gaillard with the middle bailey west wall visible. The outer skin of ashlar reveals a pattern of white and grey stripes.

the promontory. The wall facing the outer court had a cylindrical mural tower at each end, of which only foundations of the landward example survive. The rather straight section of wall on this side survives only as foundation, and at the north-eastern end is fragmentary, but it had at least one further cylindrical tower approximately half-way along its length. On the south-western (or river) side, meanwhile, a straight section pierced by five loops runs about half-way along the length of the court to a square, open-backed tower with loops at the outer angles. A short missing section then becomes an irregular length of foundation to the north-west point, where the wall angle becomes acute, almost like a beak, and runs to join the inner wall before becoming fragmentary again as the circuit is completed. Within the middle courtyard the foundations of a rectangular building, possibly a hall, abut the south-west curtain, and foundations of other buildings abutting the opposite wall are visible. Traces remain here of a possible chapel with aisle pillars and apses, seemingly overbuilt. Here there was also a well.

Within the north-western section of the middle bailey stands the inner bailey, cut off by its own ditch that runs almost entirely around it, stopping short on the north corner. The shape of this court is an irregular oval, and it consists of a curtain wall whose outer surface, where it faces into

The inner corrugated wall at Château-Gaillard, seen from the middle bailey.

Shown below from the south-western side of Château-Gaillard is the inner bailey with donjon. The foundations of the building next to the middle bailey wall on the left may be the lower room of the chapel.

the middle courtyard, is formed of close-set lobes pierced by arrow loops. This corrugated wall gives multiple fields of fire. The rear wall is plain, however, since immediately across the ditch lies the wall of the middle courtyard. These elements provide a fine example of concentric defence, the inner wall supporting the outer. The inner courtyard is reached by a bridge across the ditch, leading to a square gate-tower with small side rooms. Within this courtyard lies the last line of defence, the donjon. To the north of it, domestic ranges were butted against the curtain wall, following the slight zig-zag form of the latter.

Unlike many earlier examples set within an enceinte, Richard's donjon had already moved from lying within the enclosure to forming part of the curtain wall. It bulges out on the plain section of curtain wall, with its other side, which faces the inner courtyard, drawn out to form a massive solid stone prow, a donjon *en bec*. Internally the tower remains round: the stone prow is designed to deflect missiles aimed at it should the inner courtyard be captured, and to thicken up this area of masonry. The base of the tower is provided with a deep battered plinth. Buttresses rise up the sides, expanding as they do so, but unfortunately the top of the donjon has been destroyed. When Viollet-le-Duc attempted to reconstruct this castle in the 19th century he added battlements to the inner corrugated curtain complete with wooden hoardings. He may have been right, since it seems such a powerful fortress would not be devoid of these useful additions. However, when he similarly reconstructed the donjon, he interpreted the expanding buttresses as acting like corbels and carrying the battlements above, each

buttress joined to its neighbour by an arch. Thus he surmised that slots left in the fighting platform above the arched section allowed materials to be dropped on those below. Unfortunately this theory can neither be proved nor disproved. The donjon was entered via a door on the first floor.

Some of the surviving stone retains evidence of horizontal banding. Some outer walls feature pink or grey stone, but others do not. The donjon also has similar ashlar blocks but it is difficult to conclude that this was regular banding as the sequence does not appear to follow a set pattern.

Below the main castle, down the side of the spur on the west side, a further buttressed wall was built, to cut off an inlet in the cliff. Next to it rises a cylindrical tower built into the chalk face itself, and from here a wall foundation runs down to the river bank. Here a timber stockade stretched across the Seine to bar access to river traffic.

The donjon *en bec* at Château-Gaillard presents its solid pointed edge towards the inner bailey. The deep battered plinth is also visible, together with the deep buttresses that may have carried an early machicolated parapet. Note the use of white and grey ashlar. The entrance was to the right of the 'beak'.

FOLLOWING PAGES **Château-Gaillard**
Gaillard, the great castle built by Richard I in 1196–98, presented a formidable obstacle to an opponent. The only real line of approach was from the south, and here the attacker was met by a rock-hewn ditch and a triangular outer bailey that formed a large barbican to guard the main entrance. Richard used the latest circular towers, though the gate into this area is flanked only by a single tower. The gates connecting with the main or middle courtyard over another ditch have no supporting towers. In the middle courtyard are the domestic buildings that included a chapel, probably where the soldiers gained access via the latrine chute. Arrow loops have been added

in the crenellations, though the wall-tops have not survived. The inner ward has a corrugated wall, whose missile coverage is shown in the top left inset. Its gate was set closely between two semi-circular towers. Within is the donjon *en bec*, with a solid stone 'beak' to deter mines and deflect missiles. The top part is now missing and it is not certain if the great buttresses acted as machicolated parapets, with slots for dropping material. To the left of the castle a towered wall drops to the River Seine, and a triple line of wooden piles bars the river. In the upper right can be seen the fortified town of Petit Andely connected to the fortified Ile d'Andely. A plan view of the castle is also provided, at bottom left.

The principles of defence

The castles built by the Normans can best be seen as defended bases. On the Seine, a main artery running through the disputed Vexin territory, castles were built by both sides to try to block the other's advance. Château-Gaillard, the greatest late-12th-century castle in this area, was but one of a number of fortresses here. At Tosny, the Isle de la Tour (Boutavant) and Le Muret were forts guarding the approaches to the château. Boutavant was a quadrangular tower (of which some parts survive) on an island 5km upstream, and controlled light defences in the river to bar the Seine peninsula between Tosny and Bernières. Le Muret was a ditched motte and bailey with a circular tower on it, 2km south-east of Gaillard, in the parish of Cléry. Neaufles-Saint-Martin, built below a tributary of the Epte, was a large, deeply ditched motte and bailey castle with a donjon, which reinforced the defensive line against the French castles of Trie, Courcelles, Boury and, further down, Chaumont en Vexin.

The castles contained a number of knights and other soldiers who were trained for war, meaning that it was just as likely that the garrison would be prepared to come out and fight if they thought the odds were in their favour. At Tillières in 1119 the Norman castellan (constable), Gilbert, had his men patrol the neighbouring paths and stalled a surprise attack on the castle by surprising the French raiders instead. When King Louis advanced against Breteuil, the Norman Ralph of Gael led his cavalry out and left all the gates open to challenge the enemy to try to get in: after bitter fighting the French withdrew. The same thing happened at Falaise when Richard of Lucy dared Geoffrey of Anjou to enter: the latter declined and went off to plunder instead. This boastful attitude backfired at Le Mans, however, when the Normans in possession of the town had to retire and failed to shut the gates against the pressure of the Count of Maine's troops: the Normans barely reached the citadel.

No matter how bold the occupants, a castle had to be suitably protected, and location was a key factor. Where possible an imposing site was chosen, preferably a rocky outcrop that would deter mining. Falaise was built on such a promontory, perched on a sheer rock face leading down to the stream at its foot, removing the need for a ditch on this side. Mont Orgueil on Jersey was built on a rocky peak controlling the port of Gorey, though little 12th-century work remains today except the two chapels. La Roche Guyon began life as a fortress cut into the rock face, but in the 12th century was built up in stone. The castle at Arques (Pays de Bray) is also perched high on a long ridge overlooking the town, protected by steep ditches cut in the rock. A ravine divided the ridge, and a further courtyard would be added in the 13th century beyond this gap. On the larger site was placed the main castle, with its walls overlooking

A plan of the castle at Creully, Normandy (c.1160–70). The hall is joined to a long chamber-block of two storeys, the lower vaulting of which is shown here.

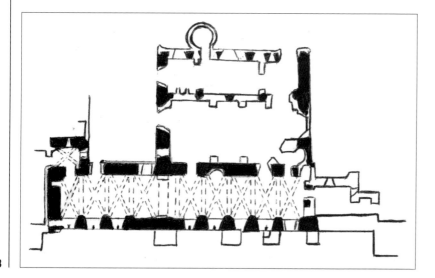

steep slopes. Another example is the castle at Saint-Saveur-le-Vicomte, which towers over the valley of the Douve below. A number of castles used other natural features to their advantage, forcing an enemy to approach from one side only, which would then be cut off by a man-made ditch. Vire stands at the central point in south-west Normandy, in the centre of a network of castles and at a crossroads. The donjon (rebuilt by Henry I in 1123) is sited on a granite outcrop bordered on two sides by the River Vire, the only access being from the north where the spur joins the plateau: the town was founded here, and served to protect the castle. At this junction a deep ditch cut the castle from the town. The town walls and towers at Vire would only be added in the 13th century though. On its spur, Tancarville made use of the Seine itself to shield one side of the castle, while at Montfort-sur-Risle the River Risle similarly protects the south-west side of the castle, which covers an area of about 280m × 165m.

At Cherbourg the area of land on which the town is situated was cut off by a moat that connected with the sea at either end. At one end of this artificial island a further section was cut off to form the area on which the castle was built. The castle was strengthened in stone during the second half of the 12th century. The donjon was enclosed in a bailey approximately 120m × 100 m, which was cut off by water from the rest of the castle. Other castles that stood by a town or city also often utilised the latter's defences. The castle at Avranches, with its slim square donjon, once stood against the south-east curtain wall of the town. At Bayeux the castle was situated in the western corner of the walls, which were later given 18 towers. The castle at Carentan was built in a bottleneck in the south-east corner of the city, though the city's defences were probably of wood until replaced by stone walls, possibly in the 13th century.

The ditches were usually dry, and were the first line of defence. When filled with rainwater and mud though, they proved significant obstacles. The stone curtain walls came next, and were at first often devoid of mural towers. Later these became increasingly common: the castle at Gisors is worthy of mention, as it preserves square, polygonal and rounded variants.

The square residential tower at the eastern corner of Tancarville castle was built in the 12th century, but the windows were altered and enlarged in 1360.

The gate at Tancarville is Romanesque, but the large flanking towers were added in 1473–78.

Early gates were simply placed within a wall, but in the 11th century the gate passage became enclosed in a tower. At Caen the gate-tower was further supported by the proximity of the donjon. Some had a portcullis. The castle at Carentan in the Cotentin, probably begun in about 1150 and popular with King John from 1199, has a square donjon with clasping corner buttresses on the eastern side of the castle enclosure, forming a gate-tower (with billet moulding) over the

The main elements of defence

The elements shown in this illustration derive mainly from the frontier fortress of Gisors in the Vexin. At top left and centre are outer (1) and inner (2) views of one of the rectangular wall towers of the second half of the 12th century. Below and to the right (3) is a semi-circular example, a late-12th-century tower liberally supplied with arrow loops, some in merlons. Below this (4) is the D-shaped Tour du Diable of 1180–90, pierced by loops. Several towers were of beaked or prow shape, with a solid stone projection to command the base of a wall through slots in the floor. The wood was protected by raw or wet hides. The supporting beams often passed through holes in the wall running along below the crenellations. In the middle left (6) is the Porte des Champs, a gate set in the wall and flanked by a rectangular tower on its right and a bastion to its left. At top right (7) is a gate-tower from nearby Château-sur-Epte, basically a passage through a tower. The large earth motte at Gisors was topped by a polygonal shell wall (8), the angles protected by shallow buttresses but with three large ones at one side. Inside was built a polygonal tower (9); the little chapel of St Thomas Becket can also be seen. The plan of Gisors (10) shows the large round tower on the far right added by Philip Augustus in the early-13th century.

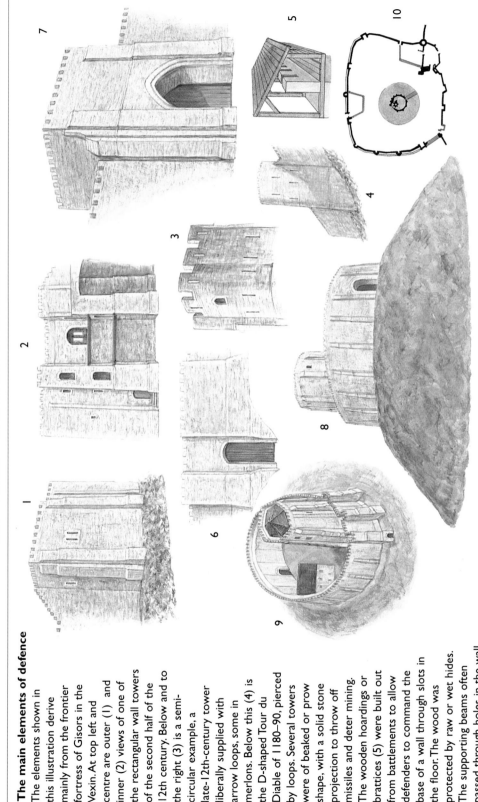

moat as well as a flanking tower. The enclosure itself was an irregular circle seemingly at that time without further mural towers. At Château-sur-Epte the bailey was surrounded in the 12th century by a stone wall with two gate-towers set with flat buttresses, with that on the plateau retaining traces of decoration. Part of the bailey was enclosed by an internal wall and connected to the motte summit by a wing wall. The internal wall has a similar gate-tower, altered in the 14th century for a drawbridge, and a second tower by the motte. This form of gate-tower became the norm until the turn of the 13th century, when the passage was itself defended by a substantial tower at either side. At Domfront the entrance is flanked by two strong polygonal towers that appear to date from the end of the 12th or beginning of the 13th centuries, probably built by the Plantagenet kings. These are the precursors of the drum or cylindrical form that would become common in the 13th century. The towers contain vaulted galleries designed to shelter archers shooting through numerous arrow loops.

A gate was accessed via the ditch and approached across a wooden bridge usually with a removable section by the door. Some of these were drawbridges, raised by means of a winch in the room over the passage, or occasionally bascule bridges, the bridge chains attached to horizontal counter-weighted beams above. A few were turning bridges, the bridge acting as a see-saw with a weighted rear end that dropped into a pit. Rarely, the stonework of the gate-tower was brought forward to form a primitive barbican.

The donjon of the 11th-century castle of Saint-Saveur-le-Vicomte may contain elements of 12th-century work; but it may also be wholly 14th century following archaic style.

The donjon was probably the last point of defence, and its imposing strength meant it was very difficult to attack. Corner and side buttresses often added to its strength, and the walls were so thick that catapults usually had little impact on them. Being of stone the tower could not easily be burned unless fire could somehow be brought to the roof, but that was usually shielded behind the upper walls and battlements. The entrance door was usually at first floor level, and the base of the walls was often provided with a battered plinth. A few late donjons (such as Château-Gaillard) were *en bec*, in which one side was drawn out to a sharp point of solid stone that was also designed to deflect missiles. Cylindrical towers of the late-12th and early-13th centuries, such as Neaufles-Saint-Martin (c.1180), with their better fields of fire and lack of vulnerable angles, were continued by Philip Augustus, as seen at Falaise. The best way to make an impression on a donjon was by mining, or to starve out those inside. Since most donjons were provided with a well and the basement was largely for storage, this too could prove a lengthy option.

However, the ability of the defenders to hit back was fairly limited. The battlements were often quite high and offered only long-range shooting. Some donjons may have had wooden hoardings fitted over the battlements, evidenced by a row of putlog holes to facilitate the fitting of the supporting beams. It may be that the remains of tall, deep buttresses at Arques and

Château-Gaillard were primitive machicolations, arched at the top and supporting battlements, allowing materials to be dropped through gaps in the parapet floor between the buttresses. However, window apertures were primarily designed for letting in light and air, and are not arrow loops as they do not possess the plunging external opening that allows an archer to depress his bow and aim towards the ground. Arrow loops do not really appear until the later 12th century. Some were placed in the merlons of battlements, splayed internally to allow an archer to angle his shot. Thus there was only so much a garrison could do once trapped in a donjon, and instances of such a siege are not particularly common.

The 11th–12th-century chapel at the castle of Crèvecoeur-en-Auge, with the bridge to the inner courtyard on the right.

The building in the inner courtyard at Crèvecoeur-en-Auge may contain a foundation of Romanesque masonry.

Château-Gaillard is an early proto-concentric castle. As noted previously, the only practical approach was via the south side, and from here an attacker was forced to capture an outer, then a middle, then an inner courtyard, the latter including the powerful donjon. It was not a true concentric design, in which inner walls follow and protect the outer walls, since this only occurs on sections of the inner and middle walls, but it utilises its setting to full advantage. La Roche-Guyon also shows this use of two curtains supporting each other, but they do not completely surround the donjon.

Life in a Norman castle

Many of the general details of daily life in a Norman castle have been covered in the first volume of this sequence, and so will not be repeated here. The focal point of any castle was the great hall (or *aula*), and was where the majority of people ate their meals, and where everyday business and local justice was conducted. Exactly what form early halls took in Normandy has been a subject of much debate. Impey suggests that the domestic complexes in Normandy between 1125 and 1225 resembled those in England. The typical arrangement consisted of an independent communal great hall at ground-floor level, open to the timber roof, associated with a residential block in two stages, The development was notably coherent, the title 'Anglo-Norman' being perhaps justified by the apparent absence of this need among non-Norman continental lords. This style perhaps developed from an Anglo-Saxon tradition already formulated, which crossed to Normandy after the Conquest. At the same time an early tradition persisted, that of storied houses, the most evident being the donjon, which was brought to England in various forms.

In the 11th century ground-floor chambers do not correspond with English models, but in the early-12th century we find two-storey stone buildings at Domfront and Vatteville-la-Rue. At Vatteville the upper stage is carried by a series of partition walls, at Domfront by an alignment of three piers.

The most impressive surviving hall, and the earliest, is that within the enceinte of Caen castle. The so-called Exchequer Hall (a 19th-century name) was 31m × 11m in surface area, perhaps the best preserved of its type in Europe, though it was badly damaged in 1944 and has been restored. The 11th- and 12th-century floor levels have been only partly preserved: this was probably a ground-floor hall, though some think that part of the area served as a kitchen, with a floor above being the principal hall. Caen had a complex of buildings in close proximity, including perhaps a chamber block. Beaumont-le-Richard in Calvados has a mid-12th-century rectangular hall with a central nave. About 10m away there is a smaller rectangular block, perhaps a solar block, consisting of a vaulted ground-floor room with a room over it, preceded by an arched ante-chamber. These buildings are aligned on the same axis. Creully in Calvados is especially similar to a type of hall often seen in England but in Normandy only at Bricquebec, Beaumont-le-Richard and Barneville-la-Bertran. It was a huge hall some 17m high, with a series of arcades separating a side aisle with a sloping roof. The hall was reworked in the 14th and 16th centuries and now has a Renaissance facade. The hall is connected to a long residential block whose outer wall also forms the rampart

Le Mont-Saint-Michel, perched on its tidal island, is a monastic fortress. Parts of the rampart on the south-west and south sides date from the 11th century, as do some western building walls and areas of the church; some buildings below the south ramparts have 12th-century work. Henry, youngest son of William the Conqueror, fled here after his father's death in 1087 to escape his brothers.

The motte at Gisors, showing the buttressed polygonal shell wall and the donjon.

The polygonal donjon at Gisors sits on the motte. Built by Henry I, Henry II added the top two storeys. The stair turret is a 15th-century addition.

wall. A two-storey building, the lower floor is vaulted throughout. The upper floor, at least, must have formed private appartments. One sees the two elements forming a coherent united structure.

Bricquebec (towards 1190) and Barneville (towards 1220) are probably the direct ancestors of the usual 13th-century dispositions, at least in England. The chamber-block forms a right angle with the high end of the hall, and it is plausible that a second chamber was superimposed at the lower end. At Bricquebec the placing of the buildings is perhaps dictated by the line of the curtain wall but their disposition approaches more a right angle than a continued axis. The chamber entrance is found in the side wall and not in the gable wall (which is the case at Beaumont). Equally important is the placing of a very small chamber above the services. This construction makes a projection in the court and had a roof forming a right angle with that of the hall; it constituted one of the cross-wings, the earliest known. At Barneville the chamber-block of the 13th century crossed the high end of the hall but was only accessed via an external stair. It is not known if a second chamber stood above the services at the lower end, as would become common.

The 11th-century Exchequer at Caen with its gable door parallels Rufus's Westminster Hall in London. The door at Beaumont is not known but at Creully it is on the extreme south of the aisle. This allows the development of the screens passage across the end of the hall, perhaps the earliest being at Oakham castle hall in England. Bricquebec and Barneville each have a service door, but the principal entrance has been lost.

The service buildings included a kitchen with ovens and hearth. Like other such buildings, the kitchen was usually separate and would sometimes remain so in later years, presumably because of the fear of fire. Kitchens are rare in donjons because important castles needed large ones to produce the quantities of food required, especially when entertaining guests. This separation meant that food came to the table warm rather than piping hot, but people would be quite used to this. Also nearby was the pantry for dry food and the buttery for wines and other drinks. At Langueuil in Seine-Maritime are 12th-century remains of a domestic building within which was a kitchen and places for tables and stone sinks. However, at Vatteville-la-Rue (Seine-Maritime), two walls remain of a domestic building, on the ground floor of which was a kitchen, cellars, store and kitchen annex. Above was a residential floor, with a large window and a door, probably to latrines overlooking the ditch.

The castle would typically contain a bakehouse, sometimes a brewhouse (in Italy and Sicily a wine

Caen castle, Normandy, c.1170

The fortress built on the ridge by the town of Caen was gradually altered over the centuries. The initial layout was that of a wall surrounding a large enclosure (1), some 266m × 233m in area.

The entrance was via a rectangular gate-tower to the north (1a). To the west an early hall (*aula*) had a chamber (*camera*) added on the east side and a chapel (*capella*) of St George at right angles. In the 1130s the castle was strengthened as shown here. Henry I added a large rectangular donjon near the gate (1b), also serving as additional protection (now only the base remains). This was augmented when he constructed a large rectangular hall, now known as the Exchequer Hall (1c), some 30m × 11m in internal area. It appears to have been a large ground-floor hall, though it has also been suggested that a kitchen on this floor served a main floor above. In the bailey stood a cistern (1d) and the Church of St George (1e). In our reconstruction the curtain walls have been provided with wooden hoardings. On the south and south-west sides especially are 11 open-backed rectangular mural towers, whose date is uncertain but which may date to the last quarter of the 12th century. The plan (2) shows the

castle with these mural towers and gates *in situ*. The northern gate-tower was destroyed in about 1220 when Philip Augustus added a large chemise and ditch around the donjon. The existing eastern gate (Porte des Champs, 2a) was added by Philip after the northern gate was pulled down.

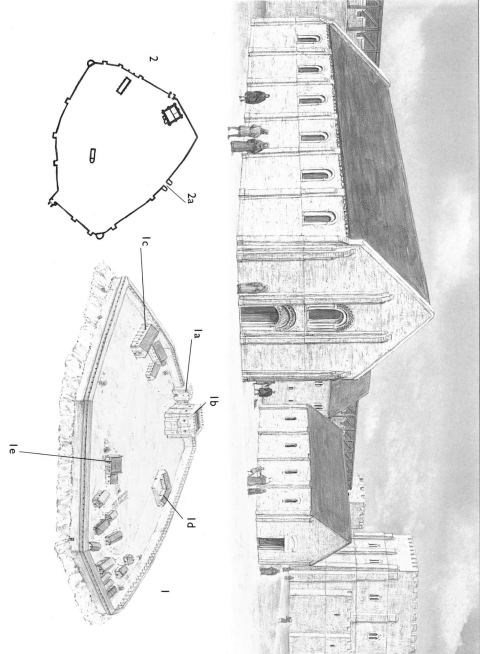

press), grain silos, barns, stables, animal pens, and possibly kennels for hunting dogs. There would also be carpenters' and smiths' shops. Many of these buildings would be timber framed with wattle and daub infills, and some might be of lean-to form. A chapel ministered to the religious needs of the castle community, and sometimes it was incorporated into the donjon itself. Others were freestanding within the bailey, such as at Crèvecoeur-en-Auge. At Condé-sur-Huisne in the canton of Rémalard, the castle has a chapel 9m by 7m in area, connected to a large room 15m × 9m via a door in the north-east wall. This room also gave access to a partly subterranean crypt, with four groined vaults radiating from a central pillar, holding up the main chapel above. This crypt may have been used as a second chapel. At Gisors Henry II built the chapel of St Thomas next to the shell wall on the motte. A priest was an important person. Since the whole community was Catholic, religious services were attended, despite the behaviour of those such as Henry II, who might be found stitching a glove while a sermon was read. However, if a man was seriously wounded, or simply old or dying of disease, a priest was needed to confess and shrive him before his end. In some castles a priest or his clerks might be the only people able to read, and this was a necessary skill if messages arrived from the duke or king. Such men might also teach young pages or squires reading skills. Though many would probably never lift a pen, it may be worth remembering Orderic's record of conversations about scripture he held with young knights in the cloisters of his monastery at Saint-Évroul. Not all knights were ignorant.

In Italian the internal domestic arrangements of castles often include the central courtyard and sometimes a square fronting the entrance, a cistern for storing rainwater (more likely than a well), buildings for corn, oil or wine, and sometimes a chapel. Residential rooms seem to have followed the pattern of the lord on the first floor and the servants on the second floor. Underground or overhead walkways frequently connected buildings, such as that between the palace and the chapel at San Gennaro at Lucito.

The number of people inside a castle varied, depending on which of the following roles it fulfilled: a marcher fortress in need of a permanently strong garrison, such as in the disputed Vexin area in Normandy; the use as a barracks

The curtain wall at Gisors, with one of the late-12th-century prow-shaped mural towers on the left.

while an army was gathered; a royal castle of the Norman kings of England and dukes of Normandy; or a small castle of a minor lord. The lord and lady of the castle would have ultimate control over its inhabitants, and they would be in charge of a wide variety of roles, as we described in the first volume. In their absence, a constable or castellan would be appointed to look after the castle. The garrison was the most important living element though. In early Normandy (at least before about 1035) the dukes were aware of the dangers of losing control of castles and careful to place *comtes* and *vicomtes* in charge of them. William the Bastard tended to choose family members as a safeguard against treachery, but this did not always work, as

The curtain at Gisors, seen from the top of the motte.

the revolt of his uncle, Count William of Arques, in 1052–53 bears out. Henry I placed his own household knights in his castles under chosen leaders to protect the surrounding areas against raiders, as at the castle at Conches in 1135. Rarely was a castle held by anyone else, except occasionally by one of the higher magnates, and these tended to be situated in areas probably less under ducal control, such as Laigle, or Échauffour. Indeed, one result of the accession of the young William the Bastard had been the revolt of western *vicomtes* who held important castles. Such men, together with certain magnates, took the opportunity to build castles, until William regained control at the Battle of Val-ès-Dunes in 1047. Orderic implies that Henry I used paid troops especially in frontier areas of the duchy. The feudal system whereby knights owed service evolved as 40 days in time of war and the same in time of peace. Garrison duty, or castle guard, in a lord's castle formed part of the duty. However, in pre-Conquest Normandy such feudal obligations were far less clearly developed than they would become in England after 1066. It is difficult to know exactly how early castles were garrisoned in Normandy. It may be that many had a number of household knights that lived with their lord and were ready at a moment's notice, similar to post-Conquest England. Also in Normandy the existence of allodial land meant these private family estates owed no service.

A similar system was employed in southern Italy and Sicily, the knights usually being present in multiples of five or ten. Not surprisingly, the early settlers brought the feudal customs of their homeland with them, until they had settled down in their new country. In about 1040 the Byzantine *theme* (provincial) armies of southern Italy were disbanded and defence was left to local urban militias (mostly Greek though some were Lombard), some of whom then went over to the Normans after their arrival. A similar reliance on urban militias was prevalent in Lombard areas, such as Capua and Benevento, while in the countryside garrisons were formed by the stronghold's owner. Some cities such as Naples had wealthy citizens who would be made knights under the Normans. Certain cities put up such an impressive defensive show

Château-sur-Epte is a motte and bailey castle in the Vexin, which was fortified in stone in the early-12th century. The gate-tower had drawbridge beam slots added in the 14th century. The cylindrical donjon on the motte rising behind the chemise was probably built by Henry II in 1184.

that the Normans allowed the citizens to continue to man their fortresses or gates. In Sicily the existing Muslim *iqta* was a form of fief that probably provided the model for smaller Sicilian feudal fees. In western Sicily the *jund* system of recruiting regional militias was continued under the Norman conquerors. On the island Lombard, Greek or Muslim villeins were expected to perform garrison service, since theoretically the Normans could summon all able-bodied men in southern Italy. Local militias gradually declined, though, especially in well-organised areas such as Sicily and Calabria. In Sicily a landed Muslim aristocracy survived until the 13th century, holding on to a number of smaller castles and provided both horse and foot throughout the period. Elsewhere the Normans gave paid employment to Muslims, and in return offered religious toleration. Muslim archers were valued for their rate of fire as well as for their agility. Equally the Muslims would provide skilled siege engineers for the reduction of obstinate fortresses or towns. Mercenaries were generally employed in all Norman areas, sometimes as part of a garrison; such men seem to have included Muslims and Lombards.

A castle projected a lord's presence and was the centre of his power. Just as the duke would favour a particular castle as a centre of his authority, his deputies, the *vicomtes*, might favour one of their own fortresses. For lesser lords, a single castle might be all they possessed. Within the hall of the fortress local justice resided, with the duke or lord overseeing court hearings and sentencing wrongdoers. Castles were also a useful place to secure political prisoners. Lords and their vassals captured in combat or simply arrested by suspicious rulers might be placed there for safekeeping, out of harm's way. Some of these men then remained in custody (in relative comfort) while their vassals and friends collected a stipulated ransom. Some prisoners fell foul of their captors simply because they were too troublesome to keep alive. The famous case of Arthur of Brittany, the nephew of King John, who was castrated and blinded while a prisoner at Falaise, is a case in point. Not surprisingly, Arthur died of his wounds.

The castles at war

Normandy

Given the turbulent history of the duchy of Normandy, it is not surprising that castles figure prominently in the struggles between the dukes and their subjects, and arising from external threats, notably from the counts of Anjou and the French kings. One of the periods of siege warfare that was to test the quality of early castles occurred after the death of Robert the Magnificent in 1035, during the first years of the rule of Duke William the Bastard, when a number of powerful nobles opposed him and set off the struggle for power that would only end when William had effectively neutralised all potential rivals. Many unauthorised castles were built, no doubt often earth and timber structures. The first milestone in his success came, with major assistance from the king of France, at the Battle of Val-ès-Dunes in 1047, which effectively broke the power of the western rebels. However, William was still not fully secure, and a number of sieges were required before he would have effective control of the duchy. Despite the persistence of several rebels, his position was now so much improved that he was able to demolish all unlicensed castles. He could now demand that no castle be erected without a licence, and expect baronial fortresses to be opened to him when required, a situation that endured for the rest of his reign.

Following the rebels' defeat, one of William's chief rivals, Guy of Burgundy, had withdrawn to his citadel of Brionne, where he continued to defy the new duke. William must have surveyed the deep ditches and ramparts of the castle, which, says his panegyrist William of Poitiers, had a stone hall that served as a donjon. William decided he was not going to risk losing men in a costly assault, but equally was not going to have his whole army tied down in one area. He ordered siege castles to be built on both sides of the River Risle, extensive earthworks within which stood wooden towers. In these defences he placed his troops, protected, as William of Poitiers notes, from sorties by the garrison. Having thus pinned down the rebel garrison he left his men to watch Brionne, and withdrew with the rest of his troops. Even so, Guy held out obstinately, his men making daily forays, and it was not until late 1049 or early 1050 that Brionne finally surrendered.

William was faced with a further threat in late summer or early autumn of 1051, when Count Geoffrey of Anjou invaded the duchy and seized Domfront and Alençon in a bid to

The donjon at Chambois was built by William de Mandeville, a vassal of Henry II, before 1189. It is 25m × 15m in surface area and almost 26m tall.

expand his power. William reacted by marching towards Domfront and then beat off Geoffrey who had confronted him. With the count sent packing back to Anjou, William built four siege castles in front of Domfront and paused. However, with no external threat now imminent, he led part of his force away one night and rode fast to reach Alençon by morning. Then, possibly insulted by the garrison's reference to the hides hanging over the ramparts and to William as the son of a tanner (his mother's family), he launched a violent assault on the town and made a breach. He then ordered retribution, the public severing of the hands and feet of those he captured. Perhaps not surprisingly, the remaining defenders wasted little time in negotiating a surrender. By the time William returned to Domfront the news had reached the garrison and they hurriedly made peace.

In the summer of 1052 Count William of Arques tried his luck and broke out in rebellion. Duke William was in the Cotentin and galloped towards the castle with a small body of men. On the way he picked up more troops from Rouen, who had tried without success to prevent Arques from being provisioned. On arriving at the castle the garrison attacked his own force but were pushed back and driven inside again. With the gates closed, the castle on its ridge presented too great an obstacle to be taken by storm, and so William resolved to build a wooden siege castle and filled this tower with men under Walter Giffard to watch the castle. William then set out to block any attempt to relieve the rebel garrison. In this his plan proved wise, for the French king, now his enemy, pushed up towards Arques, only to be ambushed by some of William's men.

Another view of the donjon at Chambois. Note the two-light windows, marking the two principal floors. The machicolated parapets were probably added in the 15th century, when the turrets were raised.

Despite this he managed to ferry some men and supplies in before being forced to withdraw: the count was left to starve slowly inside the walls. Late in 1053 he surrendered on condition his men could leave unharmed.

The three sieges by William give an interesting insight into his methods. He was cautious in assaulting a powerfully sited castle with (at least in the cases of Brionne and Arques and probably at Domfront) some stone defences. Nevertheless he was swift to seize the opportunity for a surprise move, as at Alençon. His vigorous investment of the city may, if the stories are true, have been the result of loss of temper at insults aired, but he may have decided that the defences could be breached, and the story of the hides may possibly have been invented to cover up a sudden fit of blood lust, for hides were used as a protection against fire. Whatever the truth, William quickly learned from the reactions of the men at Domfront that a brief demonstration of cruelty was worth months of passive siege. His actions at Alençon had marked him as a man to be respected, and a reputation thus achieved could only prove useful in future. Respect was always a valuable commodity in siege warfare. Henry I built up a similar reputation as a man not to be crossed, and Orderic tells us that castellans would hurriedly give up their keys when they heard that the royal army was approaching.

The three sieges do demonstrate, however, that the strength of the defences count for nothing when the enemy is determined and the supplies within the castle are limited. Notice also how the garrison of Brionne continued to launch daily attacks, while those at both Domfront and Arques rode out initially to confront William's forces; despite a strong castle they had decided to try their luck in the open. This helps to place castles in perspective and to emphasise the fact that, to a knight, honour counted for much; it could override prudence on occasion. Perhaps it was a similar scenario that allowed Geoffrey to seize Domfront so quickly, while William had chosen to starve out the Angevin intruders.

The anarchy on William's death in 1087 saw the new duke, Robert Curthose, ignored as ducal castellans were expelled by barons who took over the castles. The new king of England, Robert's brother William Rufus, was astute enough to use bribery to win over strongholds. Thus he took Aumale, Eu and Gournai on the Norman frontiers, and by this means was soon in control of much of upper Normandy. A popular rising within Rouen in favour of Rufus was only put down after much street fighting. When he came over in person in 1090 he soon reduced Robert to a treaty and they turned on their younger brother, Henry, and besieged him in his stronghold at Mont-Saint-Michel, forcing him to leave the Cotentin. Thus the castles had largely been won not by brute strength but by a cunning reading of the venal desires of the Norman barons. After Rufus's death Henry

The interior of the donjon at Chambois. The timber floor beams were carried on stone corbels, visible along the walls.

conquered the duchy in three expeditions. In 1104 he came to Domfront, which he had held for years, and placed royal garrisons in the castles whose owners he had corrupted. In 1105 he did the same in the Cotentin, but also attacked Bayeux, which he burned, and Caen, which surrendered peacefully. In 1106 he came for the third time, besieged Tinchebrai castle and was then brought to battle there by the advance of his brother, Robert, who was defeated. Once more many castles had been taken by diplomacy rather than force. But Henry also used siege-castles on occasion. Orderic mentions one at the siege of Vatteville-la-Rue in 1123–24 against Galeran de Meulan, to prevent foraging in the forest.

The conquest of Normandy by Geoffrey of Anjou between 1135 and 1145 was a matter of siege warfare rather than any major battles. In four invasions between 1135 and 1138 his fortunes see-sawed. He failed to take Le Sap in 1135, his army caught dysentery in 1137 and went home (leaving 'a trail of filth' as we are picturesquely informed), and he decided to withdraw from Falaise in 1138. However, he was able to win Fontanei in 1140, and in 1141 changed from raiding and plundering in the duchy to a methodical advance.

Geoffrey's advance against Carentan and Bayeux saw the capitulation of both without a fight. He then came to Saint Lô, which had been fortified by the Bishop of Coutances and held 200 soldiers. The latter came out to confront the Angevins but were driven back inside the defences by the first enemy attack. On the third day the defenders surrendered, and opened the gates, keen to swear homage to the count. When Geoffrey moved on the city of Coutances he entered without opposition for, says John of Marmoutier intriguingly, the

The late-12th-century cylindrical donjon at Conches-en-Ouche was set on a partly man-made motte, closely surrounded by a chemise. The donjon walls are 2.6m thick. The mural towers were added in the reign of Philip Augustus. The main area is separated from the plateau by a ditch about 20m wide and 10m deep.

bishop was away. Presumably the defenders decided they would make up their own minds when faced with a sizeable army. Geoffrey put his own garrison inside, filled the city with provisions, and called the barons of the Cotentin to do homage. One, Ralph, refused and fortified his castles while his brother, Richard de la Haye, prepared Cherbourg and installed 200 or more troops. Geoffrey in true feudal style ravaged the lands of Ralph to deny him supplies and deal out a symbolic personal insult, then took his castles and captured Ralph into the bargain. Geoffrey now marched on Cherbourg, and readied his siege engines. The walls and towers were a sight that the chronicler Marmoutier attributed to Julius Caesar; moreover he says that Richard de la Haye had filled it not only with knights, squires and retainers but plenty of provisions. For his part, Richard now ordered his men to fight well, and set off by ship to England to get help from King Stephen. Meanwhile his garrison held out stoutly and the walls and towers proved a tough nut, as missiles flew on both sides.

RIGHT **Fire-arrows at Brionne, 1092**

In 1092 a besieging force under Robert, Duke of Normandy, came to Brionne. The castle was apparently not the one that now stands on the ridge, but the earlier fortress built in the valley. When dealing with the previous siege of 1047 by Duke William, the chronicler William of Poitiers notes that Brionne possessed a stone hall, or *aula lapidea*, which served the defenders as an *arx*, or donjon, in time of trouble. This leads us to suppose that most of the buildings inside the bailey were of wood. Robert ordered the construction of a forge, and then had his archers heat arrowheads in it. The archers then aimed at the dry wooden shingles of the roof. Usually an incendiary-arrow was made by wrapping some form of cloth or tow around the shaft and setting light to it, the tell-tale smoke trails marking the progress of the missile. Now, however, the heated heads left no trail and, once lodged within the wood, they set fire to it. The defenders realised too late, and the flames took hold. Orderic was obviously impressed by this shrewd use of incendiary materials, calling it 'ingenious', which may indicate that the outer defences were also of stone, as shown here. It is also possible that they consisted of wooden palisades covered by raw or wet hides, or clay, or were plastered, since there is no reference to fire being brought to them.

The donjon at Brionne retains some of the external ashlar masonry. The castle sits in a small, arc-shaped enceinte; this may be one of two siege castle earthworks constructed by William the Bastard in 1047. A similar earthwork is found north-west of the town, on the edge of the opposite hill. In 1124 Henry I besieged Robert's son Galeran here.

Unfortunately Richard's ship was seized by pirates and he was taken away. When the news reached his men they were severely shaken, and though they had plenty of supplies (and access to ships, presumably) they decided to ask for terms before things got any worse. Geoffrey accepted their oaths of fealty, the place was handed over and, with winter approaching, the count disbanded his forces. He moved east in January 1144, crossed the Seine and advanced on Rouen. The city opened its gates but the castle held out for three months before capitulating. The last castle to be taken was Arques. Geoffrey was now duke of Normandy as well as count of Anjou. His invasion had, on the whole, been fairly bloodless and many castles offered little or no resistence to him, namely Avranches and Coutances in 1141, Verneuil and Vaudreuil in 1143, Rouen in 1144, and Arques in 1145. All these latter castles, no matter how advanced their defences, did not stand up to a siege by an army on a winning run, and with King Stephen and other leading men busy with civil wars in England, anarchy had reigned in Normandy.

Between 1173 and 1174 came a major rebellion against Geoffrey's son, Henry II, that also involved England and other areas under Angevin control. The king made sure, either in person or through his lieutenants, that castles were defensible and as safe as could be expected. In 1173 the 'Young King', together with Count Philip of Flanders, and his brother, Matthew, count of Boulogne, attacked and swiftly took Aumâle. Next he moved on Drincourt, which was stormed successfully despite being well fortified, partly through an act of treachery. He then proceeded towards Arques. In 1174 the 'Young King' and others attacked the city of Sées but were successfully held off by the citizens, despite there being no leaders present. That same year, with Louis VII of France and Count Philip, he came before Rouen on 22 July, with the Seine on their left. The outer walls were attacked in formation with siege engines but the defenders, despite being few compared to

The interior of the donjon at Brionne. The lower part contains blocked small windows and the upper embrasures, suggesting two building periods. The roof line can be seen on the upper left.

the large besieging army, forced them back by hurling square stones, sharp stakes and long pieces of wood. In order to keep up the pressure the French and Flemish took it in turn to try to undermine the walls and keep the defenders busy. This went on for several days but, says Ralph of Diceto, the Normans inside were confident they would win; their numbers were growing and food was plentiful, while men were slipping away from the siege lines for fear of starvation. Presumably surrounding lands had been torched. The final straw came with rumours that Henry II had invaded and was approaching, for Louis feared he would by-pass Rouen, invade the lands of France and attack Paris. After discussions, the besiegers burned their engines, pulled down their tents, fired their huts and other temporary buildings, and retreated from Rouen on 14 August, despite the fact that the rumours had died down. People from the border country then advanced on the furthest part of the fortification and plundered weapons and equipment.

The struggle for power between Richard I and Philip II was given a twist when Richard was captured returning from the Third Crusade. However, French barons refused to support an attack on the lands of an absent crusader. This did not stop Philip. In 1193 he invaded Normandy and seized a number of border strongholds. He advanced on Gisors, which gave up through the treachery of its castellan. He overran the Vexin and Neaufles also fell. He besieged Rouen, but the city held out because of the command of Robert, earl of Leicester, and Philip withdrew. This partial success was to prove a false dawn, however. Richard was released in 1194 and two months after his return to England was back in France. He made for the castle of Verneuil, which Philip was besieging. According to Diceto, Philip had used catapults, other siege-engines and mining to try to break into the castle, but all to little effect. Richard pushed his men into the castle, then led more men around the French rear. This was enough for Philip, and he withdrew swiftly, abandoning his siege engines in his bid to extricate himself. He took out his anger by ignoring Rouen (which he held in healthy respect) and instead besieging a small town nearby called Fontaine, which held four knights and 20 men. On the fourth day he attacked the gate, broke in and destroyed everything.

Their wariness of unpredictable open battles caused commanders to withdraw and lose a siege rather than risk all by staying to confront a relief force. Thus at the siege of Fréteval in 1194 and at Gisors in 1198, Philip Augustus abandoned the sieges rather than risk an encounter with Richard I. John was a different proposition, though his victory at Mirabeau in 1202 and capture of Arthur of Brittany led Philip to withdraw from Arques, when he was close to capturing it.

John, however, did not maintain his record; he upset a number of barons and tended to be lethargic. Philip judged his man. When he moved to seize Normandy, Anjou and Poitou from John, he fought a small river battle near Château-Gaillard but no further battles. The greatest siege of the age came in late-1203, when Philip Augustus, determined to break the rule of the English kings in Normandy once and for all, advanced against the toughest nut in the Norman duchy, Château-Gaillard. The castellan, Roger of Lacy, perhaps against his better judgement, had allowed people from the surrounding area to take refuge within the walls. Philip advanced his forces against Petit Andely and seized it, but the castle loomed over this small triumph. The king knew the only means of approach was from the south-east, and here he was opposed by the outer courtyard with its cylindrical towers, cut off by deep ditches, just as Richard had planned. A relief force arrived but was beaten off. Then Philip organised the digging of two ditches stretching from the Seine to the Gambon, to cut off the castle on the landward side and safeguard his own siege lines. He set wooden towers at intervals along the lines. Then he settled down to wait. Lacy's earlier leniency began to work in Philip's favour. As the supplies began to run low, Lacy decided there was no alternative but to turn out all those who were not necessary for the castle's defence. The 'useless mouths' were forced out of the castle to take their chances with the besiegers. At first the French complied, and we are told the first 1,000 were allowed through. Then the attitude hardened, and the route to freedom was sealed. Those who remained tried to get back inside the castle but the gates remained shut. With no prospect of immediate succour, the wretched folk were forced to huddle in the ditches through the harsh winter months, dying where they lay, tormenting the minds of those within the walls. Finally, in early 1204 Philip came up to review the situation and ordered the survivors to be allowed through and to be given food and drink. For many it was too late: on trying to digest food they succumbed.

With the coming of spring the king ordered the first direct attack on the castle. A siege tower was manoeuvred into position on the ground beyond the outer courtyard, from where French archers and crossbowmen could overlook the battlements and pin down the garrison. Catapults were brought up to pound the walls, though it is not certain whether they were torsion machines or trebuchets. Mantlets, shields of wood or wicker, were set up to protect archers and crossbowmen, while a wooden penthouse, known variously as a sow, cat or mouse, was slowly pushed forward across the ditch as men threw stones, earth and rubbish into the yawning gap to provide a causeway to allow the shed to reach the walls to protect sappers. The work was slow, and eventually the latter used ladders to descend into the ditch and up the other side to excavate a breach by the large tower. A hole was made, the inserted wooden props burned through, and a section of wall collapsed. Men swarmed across to seize the outer courtyard. The first section of the castle had fallen but there were two more courtyards and a formidable donjon still to confront. One day a soldier reconnoitering came upon the exit of an old latrine chute on the south side of the curtain of the middle courtyard. Above was a chapel butted against the wall. He managed to climb the noisome passage, emerging in the latrine below a window. Standing on a companion's shoulders he then managed to gain the window and pull some others up by rope. Once inside they made so much noise that the garrison panicked and fled, believing a large force had broken in. As they ran they fired the building. The Frenchmen opened the gates to allow their companions into the middle bailey. Next, however, they faced the corrugated inner wall. A mine was dug under it but Lacy ordered a countermine, which managed to break into the French works. However, the digging had weakened the walls and a catapult made a breach.

The donjon at Arques, built by Henry I probably after 1123, sits at the far end of the spur on which the castle is built. The deep ditches can clearly be seen.

The garrison fought on but were overwhelmed. The donjon does not appear to have been used, or perhaps the garrison was overtaken before they could retreat inside. However, it is possible that the battlements were unfinished.

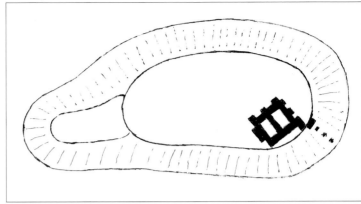

The siege of Château-Gaillard was a salutary lesson that, no matter how powerful and well garrisoned a castle may appear, it is down to the skills and willpower of the men inside and outside, and perhaps to a modicum of luck. Strong walls may hold off an attacker, but food and water would run out, especially when the local population is allowed inside for protection. As in

A plan of Arques.

other sieges, the mine was to prove lethal, and more effective than catapults. By good fortune the French found the unguarded latrine shaft, and this weak spot was used to full advantage. A slight oversight in checking the defences had cost the garrison dear. For all the ingenious design of corrugated walls and a donjon *en bec*, the French still managed to move incessantly forward and the garrison was forced to give up. The style of defence, with successive baileys and one direction of approach, might have stopped a less relentless foe, but in the end it did not save the Normans.

At Easter 1204 Philip gathered an army and attacked Falaise, which he took without resistance. The citizens of Caen similarly yielded 'for they had no-one who might defend them', states Coggeshall. Philip then took the whole province up to Barfleur, Cherbourg and Domfront. The citizens of Rouen and Verneuil and the garrison of Arques asked for 40 days in order to send messages to King John. No help came, for John feared treachery at home, and these places submitted. Normandy was lost forever.

Southern Italy and Sicily

The Norman incursions into Italy and Sicily saw periods of similar turmoil as these northern adventurers carved out territories for themselves and then attempted to hold them. In 1035 the Normans managed to gain Melfi when

The donjon at Arques was provided with deep buttresses, shown here.

their leader, the Lombard Ardoin, with his Norman followers simply persuaded the defenders to open the gates. From this already fortified mountain stronghold the Normans were able to command the country around. Many sieges were directed against native strongholds, such as Guiscard's attack on the Byzantine city of Bari in 1068, whose final capture in 1071 broke the power of the Eastern Emperor in southern Italy. Similarly, in Sicily sieges were initially directed at existing fortifications, for example the capture of Messina by Guiscard and his younger brother, Roger, in 1061. Roger, the 'Great Count', besieged Cosenza (1091), Castrovillari (1094), Amalfi (1096) and Capua (1098). It was not long before the new Norman rulers faced revolts. Robert Guiscard was

The interior of the donjon at Arques, showing the door leading to the passage to the curtain wall.

opposed by feudal factions in Apulia in 1074, 1078 and 1082. He led a swift campaign in the winter of 1078/79 to quell revolt in Calabria and Apulia, his wife Sichelgaita besieging Trani while he was dealing with Taranto. In 1084 Jordan, Count Roger's son, rebelled and took San Marco d'Alunzio, the first Norman castle on Sicilian soil. When Guiscard died in 1084 his sons and brother fought over his inheritance.

In the summer of 1062 the Greeks in Sicily rose up against the Normans. As soon as Count Roger was safely out of the way they attacked Troina, where he had spent about two weeks putting the fortifications in order and garrisoning the place. The townspeople tried to capture his lover, Judith, but the garrison beat them off in day-long street fighting, and managed to send out a messenger to Roger, who was besieging Nicosia. He came racing back, only to find that about 1,000 Muslims had joined the Greeks. Roger ordered a retreat to the citadel and the nearby streets, and barricaded the approaches. Lookouts were posted, and the siege was set. There they remained for four months, while bitter winter weather set in, all the more noticeable because of Troina's elevated position. Supplies were running dangerously low, and clothing and blankets wholly inadequate. The chronicler Malaterra says that the Normans feigned hilarity to try and keep up morale, but by early in the year 1063 Roger knew things were becoming desperate. Then the lookouts discovered that the enemy was increasingly imbibing local red wine, which helped them to keep out the cold. The Normans sized up the situation and, one night when they were reasonably sure their enemies were sleeping from the effects, seized their chance. Moving silently on the thick snow, they were able to overpower the sentries, surprise the besiegers and capture their siege lines. The ringleaders were summarily hanged, though Malaterra glosses over the fate of others.

Roger II of Sicily managed to ride the revolt against him by avoiding battle and holding his castles securely. When Guiscard's grandson, William of Apulia, died in 1127 Roger was then able to take the mainland areas as well.

When the German emperor Henry VI came down into southern Italy in 1191 Tancred spent time strengthening the defences of Sicily, the heel of Apulia and larger towns where locals preferred him to an emperor. Further north the strongholds, including Capua, hurriedly opened their gates; Salerno surrendered before Henry even arrived. Despite a pounding, Naples held out, Sicilian ships harrying his fleet and restocking the besieged citizens, until the heat forced the Germans to withdraw. Henry returned in 1194, and with Tancred now dead, Naples simply gave up. Salerno, which had given up Henry's wife (left there for safe-keeping) to her enemies as soon as he had gone home, now slammed its gates in terror but was stormed by the irate emperor; many were slaughtered, the town looted and the walls razed. As with William the Conqueror and Henry I, this lesson encouraged most other places to quickly surrender. Spinazzola and Policoro refused and suffered the same fate. Sicily was invaded and its towns and castles yielded quickly. The young heir was sent to the castle of Caltabellotta near Sciacca but the garrison lost its nerve and surrendered. On 20 November 1194 Norman rule in Sicily ended.

The fate of the castles

In Normandy the loss of the duchy to Philip Augustus in 1204 was followed by a period of construction and consolidation by the French king. He added impressive cylindrical donjons to a number of castles, including Falaise, Vernon and Lillebonne. At Caen the round mural towers are also Philip's work, and here the donjon was surrounded by its own curtain with cylindrical corner towers, the whole within ditches. Château-Gaillard was modern enough. This trend for round towers was not confined to Normandy, of course, and continued during the 13th century, but the new donjons that appeared now tended to be placed close to the front line of defences, on the enceinte rather than within it. Additional cylindrical or D-shaped towers were also built along curtain walls, as at Courcy, augmenting or replacing earlier open-backed square mural towers. Gates were now flanked by powerful towers on both sides as new and stronger gatehouses appeared. At Tancarville a Romanesque gate-tower partially survives, flanked by huge cylindrical towers erected between 1473 and 1478. As the country became gradually more ordered and the monarchy extended its authority, donjons continued to be built, though not always in the most practical defensive style of cylindrical tower: this was due to the latter's obvious internal limitations regarding domestic arrangements.

In the relatively peaceful early decades of the 14th century, before the Hundred Years War erupted, such towers were sometimes built in the old style. The square tower set on the enceinte at Saint-Saveur-le-Vicomte may look 11th or 12th century in date but most (or perhaps all) is probably later. Similarly the polygonal tower set on the motte at Bricquebec recalls the late-12th-century experimental donjons, but is considered by many to have been built in the 14th century. When the Hundred Years War broke out, castles were adapted as conditions and finances decreed; Tancarville, for example, was provided with a powerful tower on the old motte. As gunpowder gradually made its mark during the 14th and 15th centuries, towers were modified or built from scratch to carry gun ports, as occurred at Tancarville in the 1480s.

Another view of the donjon of Arques, showing the deep buttresses.

Chambois and Falaise

The great rectangular donjon at Chambois (1) was built around 1189 by William de Mandeville, a vassal of Henry II, in what was by then a rather archaic style. The tower is 25m × 15m in surface area, and 26m high, consisting of three floors. The entrance was at first-floor level via a door set in a slim tower butted against one side. In the 15th century a spiral stair was added inside the latter, but when originally built communication between floors appears to have been by ladders. The base has a battered plinth (1a). Also shown is a plan of the donjon (1b). The main floors have attractive two-light window openings and generous fireplaces. The castle of Falaise (2), birthplace of William the Conqueror, is set on a crag. The donjon was built traditionally in 1123 by Henry I, and now consists of a store cellar and a main floor containing the entrance. This was divided internally into a hall, chamber and anti-chamber, with a chapel in one corner. Several years later a second, smaller, donjon was added, presumably for additional residential space. The large bailey contained the chapel of Saint-Nicolas (2a). The southern gate flanked by two semi-circular towers (2b) may date from the second half of the 12th century. Many towers also survive on the extensive town walls, but, like some of those on the castle walls, they have been rebuilt or added later. The plan (3) shows the castle and town walls as they survive today.

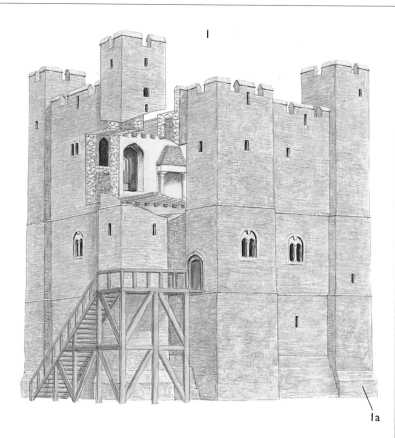

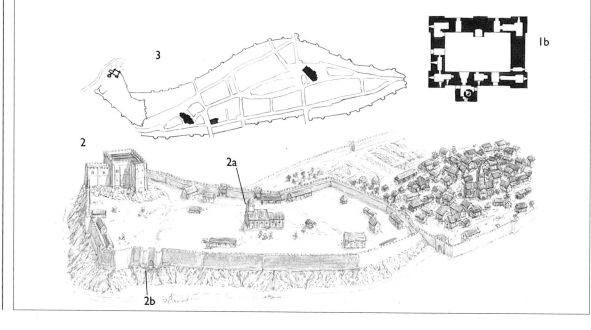

Some castles were deliberately dismantled to negate a potential threat, such as Château-Gaillard in 1603 by Henri IV. By the 17th century, however, many castles were simply redundant, as new concepts in fortification devised by men such as Vauban took over. His fortresses were not designed as luxurious châteaux but as practical defensive structures for mounting cannon and housing a working garrison. Moreover, the château became a grand residential house for the rich lord, in which the defensive aspects were neglected. Some were new, with a nod to the towers of old, while others were built on the foundations of existing castles, such as Valmont.

Many Norman castles suffered as a result. Over the centuries they were left to decay, robbed of stone by locals, so that they became the romantic ruins seen on engravings. The devastation of Normandy during the savage fighting after D-Day in June 1944 was not only grievously costly in lives but also saw the destruction of a number of historic buildings and serious damage done to many more. The clip of film of a shell bursting against Philip Augustus's tower at Falaise is unforgettable. Since then much restoration has taken place, some of it praiseworthy but in a few instances questionable. The legacy of all this means that some of the most important castles of their day are now but a shadow of their former selves. The puissant fortress at Arques is now so ruinous that several alternative reconstructions have been attempted in the past, as so much has been destroyed.

In Italy and Sicily the architectural and defensive concepts that the Norman adventurers brought with them were soon amalgamated with Lombard, Byzantine and Arabic expressions. This mixture of styles was itself to be overlaid in part by further conquerors. The influence of Emperor Frederick II of Germany meant that much architectural work in a number of earlier castles has been swallowed by his own additions. Following the Germans were the House of Aragon and Charles of Anjou; Aragonese work laid more emphasis on the palatial aspects. This overlay rather subsumed Norman work. As a result there are very few castles that show Norman work to any extent. The most impressive remains in Sicily are the palaces of La Ziza and La Cuba, which are obviously no longer Romanesque to any great degree, and whose military qualities were reduced in favour of comfort. Even here the original luxurious gardens they were set in have long been replaced by local housing and both have suffered as a consequence, especially La Cuba. In southern Italy too the ravages of time have taken their toll, and the many castles once occupied by Norman lords are often ruinous and decayed. Happily, as in Normandy, some castles were modernised, such as Pescolanciano with its cannon-ports, providing us with at least some examples of Norman work that can be visited today.

The cylindrical donjon at Neaufles-Saint-Martin, dating from the end of the 12th century, had three floors, and its walls are pierced by circular window openings (oculi). Partly ruined, the donjon was set on a motte, which was served by a large bailey.

Visiting the castles today

This chapter provides a brief guide to the key fortified Norman sites in France and Italy. The list does not claim to be comprehensive; rather it makes a selection of those most worthy of attention. The following abbreviations refer to the locations of sites, towns and cities mentioned in the following treatment.

dép.   *département* ('department', a French administrative district)
rég.   *région* ('region', a French administrative area comprising several *départements*)
prov. *provincia* ('province', an Italian administrative district)
reg.   *regione* ('region', an Italian administrative area comprising several *province*)

Normandy

Arques-la-Bataille (*dép*. Seine-Maritime, *rég*. Haute-Normandie)
About 9km south-east of Dieppe. Part of the donjon has survived. The gatehouses and some foundations in the bailey are later work, as is the outer courtyard. It was subsequently rebuilt and then destroyed in the 18th century.

Bayeux (*dép*. Calvados, *rég*. Basse-Normandie)
About 26km north-west of Caen. Now a ruin, with a donjon in the north-west corner: much of the city wall and its 18 towers are also lost. A visit to the Bayeux Tapestry is a must, as it provides examples of contemporary castles and palaces in Normandy and Brittany.

Beaumont-le-Richard (*dép*. Calvados, *rég*. Basse-Normandie)
About 20km north-west of Bayeux. In the south west of the castle a mid-12th-century rectangular great hall and residential block survive.

Bonneville-sur-Touques (*dép*. Calvados, *rég*. Basse-Normandie)
At Touques, about 2km south of Trouville-sur-Mer. Documents date it to between 1059 and 1063, and it was favoured by the dukes until 1204. An oval enclosure, it lies half-way up the valley: some parts of the ramparts reveal earlier masonry, but most of what now survives is of the 13th century. There is little evidence for a donjon.

Brionne (*dép*. Eure, *rég*. Haute-Normandie)
About 31km south-west of Rouen. The original castle in the valley was replaced by the present hill fortress (perhaps originally a siege castle). The castle is now ruinous: only two sides of the donjon survive. Earthworks to the north may be the remains of another of Duke William's siege castles.

Bricquebec (*dép*. Manche, *rég*. Basse-Normandie)
13km west of Valognes. Begun in about 1000 by the Bertrand family, this was a motte and bailey castle controlling a forest road from Valognes to the east coast. A 14th-century polygonal donjon may contain some 12th-century work, but a 12th-century hall complex survives.

Caen (*dép*. Calvados, *rég*. Basse-Normandie)
About 14km south of the ferry port of Ouistreham. The large enclosure has an impressive curtain wall set with 12th–13th-century towers, though the battlements were removed in the 17th century. Much of the original castle interior has been destroyed, including the donjon, of which only the foundations remain, set within the ditch of Philip Augustus. However, the impressive 12th-century Exchequer Hall survives. Also worth viewing is the 14th-century gatehouse.

Chambois (*dép.* Orne, *rég.* Basse-Normandie)
About 25km south-east of Falaise. The donjon is one of the best-preserved 12th-century examples in Normandy, though it is now a shell, lacking its internal floors.

Château-Gaillard (*dép.* Eure, *rég.* Haute-Normandie)
Some 40km south-east of Rouen. This huge fortress is now sadly much damaged, though it is still a very impressive ruin, particularly the ditches. The climb from Les Andelys provides good views, and there is a car park close to the castle.

Château-sur-Epte (*dép.* Eure, *rég.* Haute-Normandie)
About 50km south-east of Rouen. A delightful surviving motte crowned with a chemise and round tower, and good examples of gate-towers. The castle is now a private residence, but the interior can be seen from the gate.

Conches-en-Ouche (*dép.* Eure, *rég.* Haute-Normandie)
18km south-west of Evreux. Flanking towers were added to the exterior wall in the reign of Philip Augustus. Another D-shaped tower is a 13th- or 14th-century addition.

Condé-sur-Huisne (*dép.* Orne, *rég.* Basse-Normandie)
About 10km north of Nogent-le-Rotrou. Originally an 11th-century motte and bailey castle, a 12m-wide stone donjon plus other buildings were added in the 12th century. All of these were destroyed in 1428 except for the chapel in the north-west area.

Courcy (*dép.* Calvados, *rég.* Basse-Normandie)
About 16km north-east of Falaise. Much of the castle known to Orderic Vitalis has been reinforced, so that the stone enceinte now has 13th-century mural towers and gates. It remains a charming little stronghold set in quiet country, but is now a private farm.

Creully (*dép.* Calvados, *rég.* Basse-Normandie)
About 12km east of Bayeux. It dominates the Seulles valley. The oldest part dates from around 1060. There are remains of a 12th-century hall and a long residential building.

Crèvecoeur-en-Auge (*dép.* Calvados, *rég.* Basse-Normandie)
17km west of Lisieux. A delightful enclosure containing a number of half-timbered medieval buildings, including a 12th-century chapel. Elements of the stone tower probably remain in the later building work.

Dangu (*dép.* Eure, *rég.* Haute-Normandie)
About 8km west of Gisors. Two castles were built in the 12th century: little remains of one. The other was built on a hill west of the town, opposing the French castles of Courcelles and Boury. It features a motte surrounded by an enclosure, with a donjon built on the enclosure wall; a bailey has an enclosure wall too.

Domfront (*dép.* Orne, *rég.* Basse-Normandie)
21km south of Flers. The castle sits on a hill overlooking the town. The donjon was dismantled in about 1610 by order of the French king Henri IV. A double-aisled building once stood 20m west of the donjon, which

The castle of Courcy retains its earlier form despite the addition of the 13th-century towers seen here. A single late-11th-century square tower partly survives at the north side. In 1091 knights fought and died to protect an oven outside the castle.

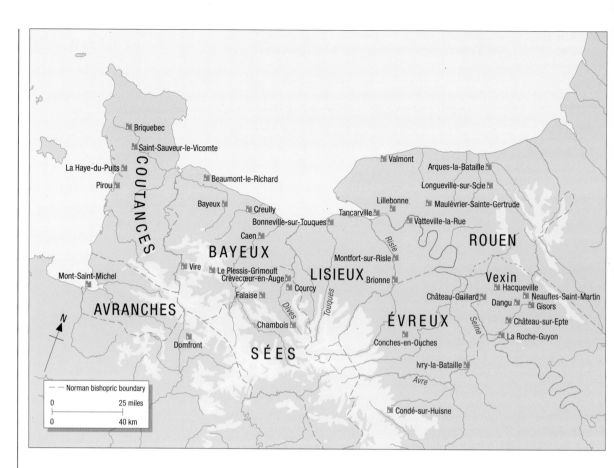

The locations of key Norman castles in Normandy. The boundaries shown indicate the Norman bishopric boundaries, as opposed to the modern-day regional and departmental zones.

perhaps was a reception *aula*. The gatehouse of c.1200 has impressive defences. Much of the castle is ruinous, including the donjon, and is overlaid by later work, but the town's defences (of mixed date) remain and make for a pleasant walk, as some towers now form part of private houses.

Falaise (*dép*. Calvados, *rég*. Basse-Normandie)
34km south-east of Caen. The birthplace of William the Conqueror, the castle was abandoned in 1617 and damaged in 1944. The rectangular donjon of Henry I has been renovated, floored and roofed, but the strange excesses (seen at the entrance especially) are wholly a matter of personal taste. Some parts of the town wall also survive.

Gisors (*dép*. Eure, *rég*. Haute-Normandie)
About 34km south-west of Beauvais. The castle is set on one side of the town, with parking next to the walls. The motte gives a good view of the rest of the castle. The walls, with their 12th-century towers of varying shapes, are an important survival though some parts are the work of Philip Augustus.

Hacqueville (*dép*. Eure, *rég*. Haute-Normandie)
About 16km north-east of Les Andelys. One of the best-preserved shell keeps in Normandy. The summit had a 12th-century wall, remains of which are included in the present farmhouse.

Ivry-la-Bataille (*dép*. Eure, *rég*. Haute-Normandie)
About 22km north of Dreux, across the River Eure. The important remains of the early donjon survive amid later work.

La Haye-du-Puits (*dép*. Manche, *rég*. Basse-Normandie)
24km west of Carentan. The castle comprises a slender quadrangular tower, with remains of a circular or polygonal wall, set on a motte. It probably dates from the 12th century, perhaps from the period of Henry I.

La Roche-Guyon (*dép.* Eure, *rég.* Haute-Normandie)

About 11km east of Vernon. It was built on the eastern bank of the Seine (between Vétheuil and Giverny) on a vertical rock set with holes. The late-12th-century cylindrical donjon *en bec* is attributed to Guy of La Roche: there are two curtain walls around it. The current entrance was built in 1780. The new fortification was connected to the old cave fortress by a subterranean stairway cut in the rock.

Le Plessis-Grimoult (*dép.* Calvados, *rég.* Basse-Normandie)

About 8km south of Aunay-sur-Orne. This site features an early earthwork and enceinte.

Lillebonne (*dép.* Seine-Maritime, *rég.* Haute-Normandie)

About 8km south-east of Bolbec. The now-destroyed hall of the castle hosted William the Conqueror's attempt to persuade his barons to invade England. The impressive cylindrical donjon is of 13th-century date.

Longueville-sur-Scie (*dép.* Seine-Maritime, *rég.* Haute-Normandie)

About 20km south of Dieppe. Lying at the bottom of the Scie valley near the town, the castle was rebuilt in the late-11th/early-12th century on top of a hill on the site of Saint-Foy priory. It was a large oval enceinte with walls but no mural towers. A wall of the gate-tower survives behind a facing wall, but there is no trace of a donjon.

Maulévrier-Sainte-Gertrude (*dép.* Seine-Maritime, *rég.* Haute-Normandie)

About 5km south of Yvetot. Known locally as 'Le Butte au Diable', the remains are to be found at the northern edge of the Caudebec forest. Probably of 11th–12th-century build, it consists of a motte encircled by a solid, levelled wall, perhaps the remains of a quadrangular donjon. The motte has a semi-circular bailey with curtain wall. A well and traces of ruined buildings survive. On the village side there is additionally an arc-shaped outer bailey whose walls cross the ditch at each end to join those of the inner bailey.

Mont-Saint-Michel (*dép.* Manche, *rég.* Basse-Normandie)

About 22km south-west of Avranches. This is a must to visit, because it is a unique fortress-monastery whose defences and buildings accumulated over the centuries. Visitors must check the tide times when crossing the causeway. It is also worth making the effort to arrive early, for the site is full of narrow streets and with many guided tours it soon becomes extremely busy.

Montfort-sur-Risle (*dép.* Eure, *rég.* Haute-Normandie)

About 14km south-east of Pont-Audemer. Built between 1035 and 1054, the donjon, whose remains lie in the south-west corner, was probably

The small castle at Pirou is a simple enclosure with no donjon. The walls are probably of late-12th century date. A single polygonal turret survives, carried on large buttresses. Where these butresses meet the wall, a triangular machicolation is formed. One can be seen on the far right of this picture.

built in 1123 by Hugh IV of Montfort, but was later confiscated by Henry I. King John dismantled parts of it, and it then fell to Philip Augustus in 1204. The castle, c.280m × 165m in area, sits on the banks of the Risle, and has a ruinous, thick-ditched, polygonal wall set with six towers of various types. The chapel of Saint Nicolas is set against the western wall of the donjon.

Neaufles-Saint-Martin (*dép.* Eure, *rég.* Haute-Normandie)
About 4km west of Gisors, Neaufles is a large, deeply ditched motte and bailey castle. The motte carries the remains of a cylindrical donjon built in the 1180s by Henry II, though the chemise wall has vanished. The donjon is 20m high and 14m in diameter, with three floors on corbels, the top floor with bonded *oculi* (circular openings). The castle was dismantled in the 17th century.

Pirou (*dép.* Manche, *rég.* Basse-Normandie)
About 27km north-west of Coutances. Pirou is a moated enceinte without a donjon. Its surviving walls and polygonal turret probably date from the late-12th century. It was rebuilt in the 14th century.

Saint-Saveur-le-Vicomte (*dép.* Manche, *rég.* Basse-Normandie)
15km south-west of Valognes, and 24km north-west of Carentan. The castle now consists of a higher court and a lower court to the south. The higher court is in the form of a lop-sided square, with a square donjon attached to, and jutting from, the south-east corner. This appears to be of 14th-century date but may be an altered 12th-century original. All the mural towers along the walls of the high court are round and of the 13th century, while only a few remnants of the lower-court defences remain.

Tancarville (*dép.* Seine-Maritime, *rég.* Haute-Normandie)
About 12km south of Bolbec. The 12th-century Norman tower remains at the south corner of this long triangular castle enclosure overlooking the Seine. A smaller square tower, flanking the ramp leading to a huge beaked 15th-century tower, may also be of 12th-century date.

Valmont (*dép.* Seine-Maritime, *rég.* Haute-Normandie)
About 11km south-east of Fécamp. The early square donjon is now amalgamated into the later château but is clearly visible at one corner. The castle is relatively compact and follows the line of the original layout, though one half is largely missing. There is also extensive parkland.

Vatteville-la-Rue (*dép.* Seine-Maritime, *rég.* Haute-Normandie)
About 15km south-east of Lillebonne, across the Seine. The castle consists of a motte with remains of a polygonal shell-keep on top. Across the ditch, to the east, is a crescent-shaped bank with remains: excavation has shown this to be a residential building. The motte south of Vatteville on Route 65 is perhaps the siege-castle built by Henry I in 1123–24.

Vire (*dép.* Calvados, *rég.* Basse-Normandie)
54km south-west of Caen, and 26km west of Condé-Sur-Noireau. The castle is easily reached from the town, with the donjon rearing up on its rocky base. It was dismantled by Richelieu in 1630 and collapsed in 1802.

Southern Italy

Bovino (*prov.* Foggia, *reg.* Apulia)
Bovino stands south of the River Fortore. It was built either by the Norman Drogone, or by the counts of Loritello, on Roman remains.

Campobasso (provincial capital, *reg.* Molise)
Located on a high spur over the town, the castle was erected by the Normans on the site of a Lombard tower, which contains remains of Samnite walls beneath. The castle was four-sided, with a donjon situated between the northern and western sides. Four circular corner towers were added later.

Castel d'Arechi (*prov.* Salerno, *reg.* Campania)
Situated at an elevation of 300m on Mt Bonadies, the site was developed and fortified by Arechi II, a Lombard prince. In 1077, following a lengthy Norman siege, the castle was taken from Gisulfo II, the last Lombard prince of Salerno. The site was much altered in the 16th century, and abandoned in the 19th century.

Castel Bagnoli del Trigno (*prov.* Isernia, *reg.* Molise)
A four-sided Langobard castle on a rocky spur overlooking the Trigno river valley. The Normans raised escarped walls, with three sides slightly overhanging: the wall with the entrance overhands more prominently. Internal arrangements against the inner walls have decayed and what appear to be cannon loops have been inserted in the remains.

Castel dell'Ovo (*prov.* Naples, *reg.* Campania)
The Normans chose the site for their base in the 12th century, and commissioned the architect Buono to expand and improve the existing shore fortifications. The 'Normandy' tower dates from this period. The site was altered once more under the Swabians.

Castropignano (*prov.* Campobasso, *reg.* Molise)
Castropignano lies about 20km from the regional and provincial capital, Campobasso. The four-sided castle itself sits on a rocky ridge and was originally a Langobard fortress, which the Normans rebuilt to include a donjon and towers.

Conversano (*prov.* Bari, *reg.* Apulia)
The town is about 18km from Monopoli. The castle was built on a preceding Byzantine structure. It is of trapezoid form and three of the 12th-century square towers survive, together with a cylindrical 14th-century example. It was restructured by Frederick II in 1230. There is an archaeological museum within the castle.

Deliceto (*prov.* Foggia, *reg.* Apulia)
Deliceto is located 50km from Foggia, and the town sits on a hill at an elevation of 550m. The castle was erected in 1073 by the Norman Tristainus.

Dragonara (*prov.* Foggia, *reg.* Apulia)
The castle was built, probably on Roman remains, by Drogone Count of Apulia, the second son of Tancredi, from whom it derives its name.

Fiorentino (*prov.* Foggia, *reg.* Apulia)
The city is famous for being the place where the emperor Frederick II died on 13 December 1250. The Normans expanded the city considerably, adding a suburb called the 'Carunculum', and erected a small castle on the highest point of the hill. The castle was later altered by Frederick II.

Longano (*prov.* Isernia, *reg.* Molise)
Located about 10km from Isernia, in the Matese highlands. The castle overlooks an elongated township. Little remains of the enceinte, much of the stone having been pillaged for urban construction, and controversy exists over the precise date of foundation.

Melfi (*prov.* Potenza, *reg.* Basilicata)
The town of Melfi was taken by the Normans in 1041 and was their first capital in southern Italy. Remains of a Norman rectangular donjon

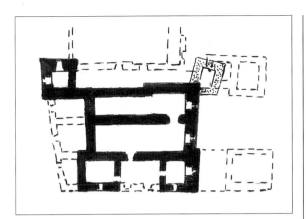

The donjon at Melfi has an internal cross wall but the building has become rather encased in later work, shown in the plan above as broken lines. A lost 12th-century tower once stood at the top right corner of the donjon.

The castle of Melfi was the first to be taken over by the Normans. The rectangular donjon was built in the late-11th century but is now enclosed. Part of it can just be seen above the 13th-century curtain walls.

The walled city of Mdina in Malta was already a fortified stronghold when Count Roger arrived before it in 1090. Some traces of the Muslim and later work may remain in the curtain walls.

are visible, though the castle was heavily rebuilt in 1281 and badly damaged in an earthquake in 1851.

Monteroduni (*prov.* Isernia, *reg.* Molise)

The castle is located on the slopes of Mount Altone, near the River Volturno. The Langobard defences were overlaid in later centuries. In 1064 it was taken over by the counts of Molise on the deaths of Bernardo I and his sons in battle against the Normans. Very probably in the Norman period, the small courtyard enceinte was given four corner towers, but much of the castle was heavily altered in the centuries that followed.

Mount Sant'Angelo (*prov.* Foggia, *reg.* Apulia)

The castle lies to the west of the town itself, and is now in a ruinous state. The pentagonal Tower of Giants was erected by Robert Guiscard.

Nicotera (*prov.* Cosenza, *reg.* Calabria)

The castle was built in 1065 by Robert Guiscard, but was destroyed in 1074. Count Roger, having been granted Nicotera in a will, rebuilt it and transfered his *domus regia* and *praedia regis* there. However, it was destroyed again in 1085. It was rebuilt again in 1122 by the young Count Roger, but suffered an earthquake in 1184. It was much altered by Frederick II and rebuilt in the 18th century. The castle contains several museums.

Pesche (*prov.* Isernia, *reg.* Molise)

A fortified burgh on Mount San Bernardo. The village is surrounded by a curtain set with cylindrical corner and middle towers, making the buildings an initial obstacle to attack. Behind rises the castle, with a redoubt like a small donjon on an escarped base. This enceinte and redoubt are more like Abruzzi castle forms, and are not common in the Molise region.

Pescolanciano (*prov.* Isernia, *reg.* Molise)

Situated on a rocky spur, the castle has a trapezoid floor plan and features a four-sided donjon (possibly Norman). Frederick II removed much early work, as he did in other Molisian castles. Much rebuilding has taken place at the site.

Riccia (*prov.* Campobasso, *reg.* Molise)

The town is some 32km from Campobasso. The castle is located on the eastern side of two hills, overlooking the valley formed between them. It has an irregular enceinte with three circular towers (one almost vanished) and a cylindrical donjon of basement and three storeys.

Roccamandolfi (*prov.* Isernia, *reg.* Molise)

Located some 23km from Isernia, the castle (originally called Rocca Maginulfi) sits on a hilltop overlooking the town. It was destroyed by

Frederick II, and only ruins remain. The enceinte, featuring somewhat later cylindrical and D-shaped mural towers, follows the irregular hillside and on two sides incorporates a four-sided structure, possibly a donjon.

Rotello (*prov.* Campobasso, *reg.* Molise)

Founded by Robert of Loritello (grandson of Robert Guiscard) from whom it derived its name: the castle currently goes under the name of Palazzo Colavecchio, and is situated in the centre of the village. Although it has been much altered, its structurally dissimilar elements seem to indicate an earlier Norman building.

San Marco Argentano (*prov.* Cosenza, *reg.* Calabria)

Located some 50km from Cosenza, the castle was built by Robert Guiscard in 1051, including a stone donjon, and rises to dominate the whole valley. Interestingly, the so-called 'Norman tower' was in fact built in the late-Swabian period, or may indeed date to the 14th century.

Scribla (*prov.* Cosenza, *reg.* Calabria)

The site lies in northern Calabria, a few kilometres south-east of the city of Castrovillari. Built by Robert Guiscard, probably between 1044 and 1048 (the first date is provided by Lupus Protospadarius, while the second is by Goffredo Malaterra). Archaeological research has indicated that the site was abandoned for a period of ten years, before being reoccupied. It featured a trapezoid wall with a tower on its east side.

Termoli (*prov.* Campobasso, *reg.* Molise)

In the Norman period the Langobard tower was rebuilt and incorporated into an expanded defence system. There was probably an enceinte and possibly a donjon before Frederick II rebuilt the place. Within the city is the *palatium* of the Loritellos, where Tancred finalised an agreement against Henry VI in 1191.

Tremiti Islands (*prov.* Foggia, *reg.* Apulia)

The fortress here features a long ramp leading up to a gate, and high escarped walls on bedrock. The Tower of St Nicholas protected the artificial ditch that separated the citadel from the north-eastern side of the island.

Tufara (*prov.* Campobasso, *reg.* Molise)

A castle in the County of Civitate, it owed the king the service of a soldier. In the mid-12th century it belonged to Drumanus. Traces of piling from the original wooden defences have been discovered. The shape is elongated and kinked, the length probably due to successive building. During the Norman period there seems to have been reworking on the

The castle of Caccamo in Sicily.

south-east side, where it overlooked the Celano–Foggia route and the River Fortore. The creation of the block that houses the armoury can probably also be traced back to Norman rebuilding work.

Venafro (*prov.* Isernia, *reg.* Molise)

The castle stands on the edge of the town on the hill of Sant'Angelo. Its cylindrical donjon was built over the course of several centuries on top of a pre-Roman structure.

Sicily

Aci Castello (*prov.* Catania)

The castle, of black lavastone, sits on a spur overlooking the sea on a site that had been fortified since the Roman period. It was rebuilt by Tancred in 1189.

Adrano (*prov.* Catania)

This is an early, square donjon surrounded by a later low chemise wall with circular corner towers. Other elements of the castle complex are of later date.

Caccamo (*prov.* Palermo)

The castle is perched high on a ridge of Mount Calogero, about 14km from Termini Imerese, south-west of Cefalù. It was built by a rich Norman called Matthew Bonnellus. The castle has been much rebuilt and restored.

Calascibetta (*prov.* Enna)

The town is some 6km to the north of Enna, and lies at a quota of 691m in the Erei mountains. The town's name is of Arabic origin (Kalat-Scibet), and means 'the castle on the summit'. In 1062 Count Roger built a castle and church here.

Caltabellotta (*prov.* Agrigento)

The site has a single Norman tower surviving which stands on a hill at an altitude of 950m. The castle was built on the site of a former Arab castle. It was here in 1194 that the widow Sybil took refuge together with her son William III from the pursuit of the Swabian emperor Henry VI.

Lentini (*prov.* Siracusa)

The town lies at a height of 56m, and is some 45km from the provincial capital Siracusa. The Arabs fortified the town, before it fell to the Normans. The town suffered earthquakes in 1140 and 1169, which destroyed many buildings of the period. The site of the castle was overlaid by Frederick II.

Mazara del Vallo (*prov.* Trapani)

The town is on the west coast of Sicily, some 40km south of Trapani. The site was fortified by Roger I in 1072–73, to protect against the Saracen invasions. The first Sicilian parliament was held here soon after. Only its double-arched entrance remains, near Piazza Makara.

Milazzo (*prov.* Messina)

The city lies 40km west of Messina. The oldest part of the site is the 'Mastio', which is known as the 'Saracen Tower'. The castle was heavily reworked in 1240 by Richard of Lentini for Frederick II.

Palermo: Castellaccio

Perched on Monte Caputo, and built in the second half of the 12th century, the site forms a large irregular rectangle, with rectangular towers. The

The remains of the 11th–12th-century Torre Pisano in the fortified palace of the Norman kings of Sicily at Palermo is austere, despite the decorated windows.

ground plan of a square donjon with a dividing wall still exists.

Palermo: La Cuba

This palace-tower was built by King William II in 1180, and was set in a large park, which also contained another building, 'La Cubula' (see below). It now stands in the grounds of the Villa di Napoli, on Corso Calatafimi, through which access is gained.

Palermo: La Cubula

The building is located on Corso Calatafimi, near to La Cuba: once again, access is via Villa di Napoli.

Palermo: La Ziza

La Ziza lies in the north-west part of the Sicilian capital in Piazza Guglielmo il Buono, near Porta Nuova. It was begun by William I in about 1162, and was completed by his son, William II. Today it contains a museum of Islamic art.

Palermo: Palazzo Conte Federico

Via dei Biscottari. Arab-Norman work survives in the tower of this palazzo, called the 'Scrigno Tower': it is now a private building.

Paternò (*prov.* Catania)

Located 13km from Catania, the lavastone castle, which dominates the town, was built by Roger I in 1073 and rebuilt in the 14th century. It has been much restored in recent years. The castle is open to visitors daily.

Termini Imerese (*prov.* Palermo)

The castle lies in the upper part of this thermal spa town, which is 36km from Palermo. The site is an ancient one, stretching back to classical times, and its use was continued by the Normans following their takeover in the 13th century. The castle was overlaid by Frederick II.

Trapani (provincial capital)

The castle lies on an ancient site on the summit of Mt Erice, and provides excellent views down over the city. In the 12th century the Normans used materials from existing structures to build a castle and curtain wall with numerous entrances and gates. The original site, more extensive than today's remains indicate, contained an outer ditch with three towers in advanced positions: this area was connected to the main castle via a drawbridge.

The Norman palace building of La Cuba, in Palermo, Sicily. It once formed part of a large park in the city. (By kind permission of Dr David Nicolle)

The church of San Giovanni dei Lebbrosi is part of the hospital converted from the small fort that stood on the edges of Palermo. It was first seized by Count Roger before his attack on the city itself: he made it into a castle.

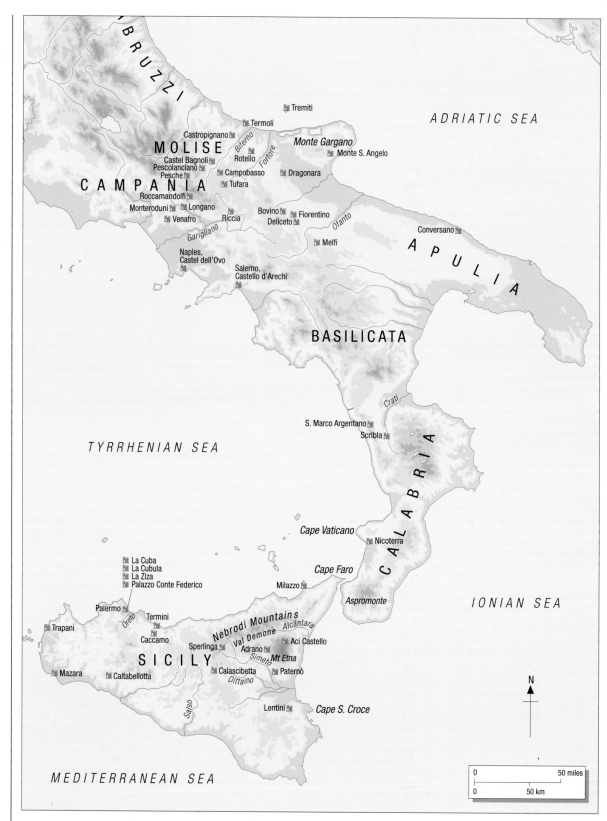

The key Norman castles and sites in southern Italy and Sicily. The regional names given refer to the modern Italian boundaries, as opposed to historical demarcations.

Bibliography

Allen Brown, R (ed.) *Castles: A History and Guide* (London, 1980)
    The Architecture of Castles (London, 1984)
Anderson, WFD *Castles of Europe* (London, 1970)
Baylé, M (ed.) *L'Architecture Normand au Moyen Age*, 2 vols (Caen, 2001)
Beck, Bernard *Châteaux Forts de Normandie* (Rennes, 1986)
de Boüard, M *Le Château de Caen* (Caen, 1979)
    Les Châteaux Normands de Guillaume le Conquérant à Richard Coeur de Lion,
    exposition, Musée de Normandie (Caen, 1987)
Bradbury, J *The Medieval Siege* (Woodbridge, 1992)
Caronia, G. *La Ziza di Palermo: storia e restauro* (Bari, 1982)
Caronia, G. and Noto, V. *La Cuba di Palermo: Arabi e Normanni nel XII° secolo*
    (Palermo, 1988)
Châtelain, André *Donjons romans des Pays d'Ouest* (Paris, 1973)
    Châteaux Forts, Images de Pierre des Guerres Médiévales (Paris, 1995)
Clapham, AW *Romanesque Architecture in Western Europe* (Oxford, 1936)
Counihan, JM 'Mrs Ella Armitage, John Horace Round, G.T. Clark and Early
    Norman Castles', *Anglo-Norman Studies*, Vol. VIII, pp73–87 (1986)
Davison, BK 'The Origins of the Castle in England', *Archaeological Journal*, Vol.
    CXXIV, pp202–11 (1967)
    'A survey of the Castle of Arques-la-Bataille, Seine Maritime', *Journal of the*
    British Archaeological Association, 3, Vol. xxxvi (1973)
Douglas, DC *The Norman Achievement* (London, 1969)
Gauthiez, B 'Hypothèses sur la Fortification de Rouen au Onzième Siècle. Le
    Donjon, la Tour de Richard II et l'Enceinte de Guillaume', *Anglo-Norman*
    Studies, XIV (1991)
Gies, J and Gies, F *Life in a Medieval Castle* (London, 1975)
Gravett, C 'Siege Warfare in Orderic Vitalis', *Royal Armouries Journal*, Vol. V,
    pp139–47 (Leeds, 2000)
    The History of Castles (Guilford, CT, 2001)
Impey, E 'The Seigneurial Residence in Normandy, 1125–1225: an Anglo-
    Norman Tradition?', *Medieval Archaeology*, Vol. 43 (1999)
Kenyon, JR *Medieval Fortifications* (Leicester, 1990)
Mesqui, J *Châteaux et Enceintes de la France Médiéval*, 2 vols (Paris, 1992–93)
    Châteaux Forts et Fortifications en France (Paris, 2002)
Norwich, JJ *The Normans in the South, 1016–1130* (London, 1967)
    The Kingdom in the Sun (London, 1970)
Platt, C *The Castle in Medieval England and Wales* (London, 1982)
Renoux, A 'Châteaux et résidences fortifiées des ducs de Normandie aux Xe et
    XIe s.', *Les Mondes Normandes (VIIIe–XIIe s.): actes du IIe congrès international*
    d'archéologie médiévale, pp113–124 (Caen, 1989)
Thompson, MW *The Rise of the Castle* (Cambridge, 1991)
    'The Military Interpretation of Castles', *Archaeological Journal*, Vol. CLI,
    pp439–45 (1994)
Toy, S *Castles: Their Construction and History* (London, 1939)
Tuulse, A. *Castles of the Western World* (London, 1958)
Yver, J 'Les Châteaux-Forts en Normandie jusqu'au Milieu de XIIe Siècle',
    Bulletin Soc. Des Antiquaires de Normandie, Vol. liii (1955-6)
Zadora-Rio, E 'L'Enceinte Fortifié du Plessis-Grimoult, Résidence Seigneuriale
    du XIe Siècle', *Château-Gaillard*, Vol. V (1970)

Index

See also lists of other castles in 'Visiting the castles today'

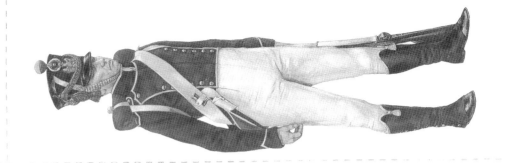

FIND OUT MORE ABOUT OSPREY

❏ Please send me the latest listing of Osprey's publications

❏ I would like to subscribe to Osprey's e-mail newsletter

Title / rank

Name

Address

City / county

Postcode / zip   state / country

e-mail

FOR

I am interested in:

❏ Ancient world
❏ Medieval world
❏ 16th century
❏ 17th century
❏ 18th century
❏ Napoleonic
❏ 19th century

❏ American Civil War
❏ World War 1
❏ World War 2
❏ Modern warfare
❏ Military aviation
❏ Naval warfare

Please send to:

North America:
Osprey Direct , 2427 Bond Street, University Park, IL 60466, USA

UK, Europe and rest of world:
Osprey Direct UK, P.O. Box 140, Wellingborough, Northants, NN8 2FA, United Kingdom

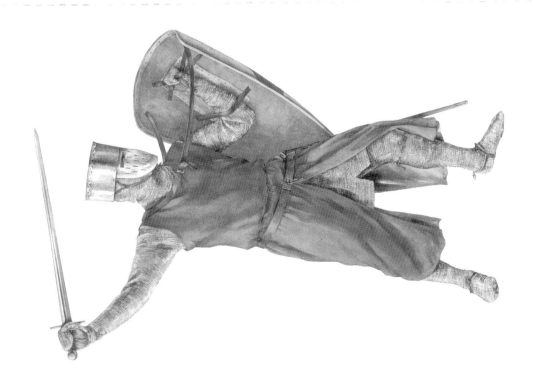

OSPREY
PUBLISHING

www.ospreypublishing.com

call our telephone hotline
for a free information pack

USA & Canada: 1-866-620-6941
UK, Europe and rest of world call:
+44 (0) 1933 443 863

Young Guardsman
Figure taken from *Warrior 22:
Imperial Guardsman 1799–1815*
Published by Osprey
Illustrated by Richard Hook

Knight, c.1190
Figure taken from *Warrior 1: Norman Knight 950 – 1204 AD*
Published by Osprey
Illustrated by Christa Hook

POSTCARD